CAPITAL BUDGETING

CAPITAL

BUDGETING

TOP-MANAGEMENT POLICY ON
PLANT, EQUIPMENT, AND
PRODUCT DEVELOPMENT

By JOEL DEAN

GRADUATE SCHOOL OF BUSINESS, COLUMBIA
UNIVERSITY, AND JOEL DEAN ASSOCIATES

NEW YORK AND LONDON
COLUMBIA UNIVERSITY PRESS

PREFACE

Making decisions on capital expenditures is one of the most demanding responsibilities of top management. There are few guideposts for determining either the amount or the kind of investments to make. Without such guides, decisions are made on the basis of ill-defined standards and intuitive judgment. There is a need for an analytical framework that will systematize management's approach to this problem.

This book makes a beginning at filling this need by developing an economic approach to executive decisions on internal investments. It does not pretend to be a comprehensive survey of all capital budgeting problems, since relatively little attention is given to procedures and administrative routines. The main emphasis is on substantive issues of getting and spending capital.

The practical capital budgeting experience of several large corporations was a point of departure in developing the analysis presented here. I have learned much from my clients, and I am indebted to the Socony-Vacuum Oil Company for permission to publish ideas that were worked out for their private use. Executives of the following companies have contributed to my education in these matters: Celotex Corporation, Chesapeake and Ohio Railway Company, Flintkote Company, General Electric Company, General Motors Corporation, Gulf Oil

Corporation, Johns-Manville Corporation, Shell Oil Company, and Standard Oil Company (New Jersey).

In preparing this monograph, I have had the able assistance of Stephen Taylor and Philip Brooks of Joel Dean Associates. Mr. Taylor worked with me at every stage of the preparation, editing and revising my drafts and making major contributions to the analysis. He also cheerfully shouldered the onerous burden of revising the proofs. Mr. Brooks was also of major assistance in developing the analysis, in the course of our work with clients, and he reviewed the entire manuscript.

It is a pleasure to acknowledge the kindness of the following persons in reading the manuscript: James Bonbright, Albert Hart, Michael Gort, and Wilson Payne, Columbia University; Melvin de Chazeau, Cornell University; Frederick Donner, General Motors Corporation; John Kusik, Chesapeake and Ohio Railway Company; A. L. Nickerson, Socony-Vacuum Oil Company; Dexter Keezer, McGraw-Hill Publishing Company; and Theodore Yntema, Ford Motor Company. Mary Hudson competently and patiently typed the manuscript through many drafts.

J.D.

NEW YORK CITY
MARCH, 1951

CONTENTS

CONTENTS

CHARTS

TABLES

Chapter I

INTRODUCTION

THIS BOOK is concerned with the economics of capital budgeting—that is, the kind of thinking that is necessary to design and carry through a systematic program for investing stockholders' money. Planning and control of capital expenditures is the basic top-management function, since management is originally hired to take control of stockholders' funds and to maximize their earning power. In a broad sense, therefore, product-line policy, promotion, pricing, and labor relations can be viewed as subsidiary problems of administering management's trusteeship over capital.

The scale on which management spends investors' money is reflected in Chart 1, which shows total non-farm investment expenditures in durable plant and equipment. This chart understates the role of capital budgeting, since, as shown later, investment expenditures go far beyond outlays on durable plant. But investments that take less tangible form, for example, outlays to build a dealer organization, are expensed by conventional accounting practices and are thus hidden among the operating expenses. Panels B and C show that visible business expenditures are much more volatile than gross national product but considerably more stable than other private investment, such as house construction and inventory changes. Private investment is a more strategic factor in the level of business activity than its percentage of the national product would indicate. Investment decisions depend on more sophisticated and more long-run views of future prospects than consumption expenditures do and are less closely tied to the current level of income. Hence, management in its capital budgeting is an independent source of demand for labor; its decisions to invest have important consequences for general income levels. Chapter X examines, from a managerial viewpoint, capital budgeting policies that are aimed at damping these fluctuations in outlay.

Although capital budgeting is conceptually, at least, the universal business problem, encompassing all others, few executives are happy with their own solutions to it. Capital budget reviews take too much time, and without systematic rejection and acceptance criteria, the pivotal decision on the size of the total expenditure that should be authorized in a given year has no solid foundation. Allocation of funds among projects, moreover, is often determined by skill and persistence of persuasion rather than by objective indexes of company welfare. This book is a broad-gauge view of a system for capital budgeting founded on economic analysis and designed to reduce the executive time and confusion involved in making decisions. The system is offered tentatively, because until recently capital budgeting has had little attention by economists, and there exists a no man's land between the pure theory of investment and management's decision to spend.

Chart 1

Dollar expenditures shown are for non-farm producers, domestic plant and equipment gross, before allowances for depreciation. These expenditures were greater than total private investment in 1932–1934 because the total reflects large inventory disinvestments in those years. The averages shown are ratios of the 21-year totals of investment and national product.

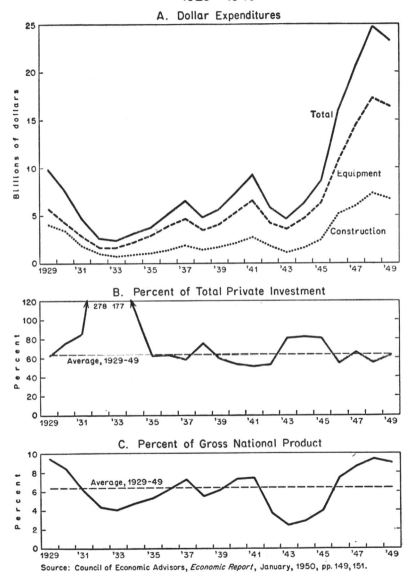

Chart 1
Private Business Investment in the United States
1929 – 1949

A. Dollar Expenditures

Total

Equipment

Construction

B. Percent of Total Private Investment

278 177

Average, 1929-49

C. Percent of Gross National Product

Average, 1929-49

Source: Council of Economic Advisors, *Economic Report*, January, 1950, pp. 149, 151.

MEANING OF CAPITAL EXPENDITURE

A capital expenditure should be defined in terms of economic behavior, rather than in terms of accounting conventions or tax law. The criterion, then, is the flexibility of the commitment involved, that is, the rate of turnover into cash.[1] For instance, inventories and receivables, although assets on the balance sheet, turn over fast enough to make their level fairly adjustable to short-run changes in outlook. They are, therefore, excluded from the capital budget. Major replacements or additions to plant capacity, on the other hand, take several years to return their cash outlay. Their value to the company during this period is usually much above the amount they could be sold for—that is, they tie up capital inflexibly for long periods. They involve more uncertainty, forecasting judgment, and company-wide thinking than an inventory investment does and justify a special procedure for management review. The same is largely true for major research on new products and methods and for advertising that has cumulative effects. Costs of educating executives and developing dependable distribution connections fall into the same category.

Obviously, this definition of outlays that budget as capital expenditures does not accord well with the accounting distinction between capitalized and expensed outlays. Although it includes most items capitalized by accountants, it also includes some important expenditures that are usually expensed by accountants, such as long-term advertising, training, and research. The disparity hinges largely on the tangibility of an asset rather than its economic nature, and the need for controls and conventions in accounting is contrasted with the econ-

[1] In practice, an exception must be made for minute outlays, regardless of how slow to cash.

omist's intellectual license. The broader definition is needed in making business decisions, even though some investments— for example, cumulative advertising—cannot be measured neatly either in amount or in productivity.

CAPITAL BUDGETING PROCEDURE

The budgeting problem may be made quite clear by running through a budgeting procedure for a one-year plan and noting what kind of answer is wanted at each stage.

The head office first asks divisions for a list of capital expenditure "needs" or proposals for the coming year. These requests for capital stack up to $20 million.

An estimate is next made of the cash that will be available for these outlays. It appears that depreciation charges will total $5 million and that net income will be $10 million. But management wants to pay a $5 million dividend. Thus, internally generated cash available for investment is $10 million. A $4 million term loan is feasible, though no public financing is contemplated, so available funds apparently total $14 million.

			Millions of Dollars
Capital Needs			20
Capital Supply			
Depreciation	5		
Net Income	10		
Cash Generated	15		
Less Dividend	− 5		
Net Internal Supply		10	
Borrowing	4		
Equity Financing	0		
Net External Supply		4	
Total Capital Supply			14
Cut-back Required			6

Management at this point has two questions to answer. First, are these proposals promising enough to warrant borrowing the $4 million or perhaps even retaining the $5 million of earnings? Indeed, are they superior to investing depreciation charges in municipal bonds? Second, on the assumption that all $20 million of the requests are good proposals, how should the best $14 million of them be selected to invest the available funds?

There is a further question of major importance to ask of all proposals: Is this the best time to make this investment, or will its value ripen if it is postponed?

BUDGETING PROBLEMS

Four aspects of capital budgeting are to be discussed in this book—the demand for capital, the available supply, its rationing, and the timing of its use. The nature of the central question which is posed by each aspect needs to be examined here.

Demand (Chapter II). How much money in total will be needed for capital expenditures during the coming period?

Since the objective of capital expenditures is to make profits, "need" should be measured by prospective profitability. Thus this problem involves a survey of opportunities for profitable internal investment and implies some system of screening requests on the basis of prospective profitability.

The problem therefore requires methods for estimating the prospective return on proposed capital expenditures. A few general principles that underlie every profitability estimate should be kept clearly in mind. Estimates that differ in refinement will be made at various stages in the development of a proposal, and different kinds of estimates will be required for different kinds of investments (e.g., cost-saving investments versus expansion investments). Moreover, the precision with which prospective return can be guessed will vary greatly among proposals. Nevertheless, it is important that the conceptual framework of estimating be correct and that the form of profit estimates be uniform for all proposals.

Since errors are unavoidable, they raise the problem of making some allowance for differences in precision of estimates for various types of proposals. Differences in precision arise from varying uncertainty as to whether assumed conditions will ever appear; they are also caused by strategic benefits that vary among investments. Both uncertain and broad-gauge investments must be further processed if they are to be fitted into the budgeting scheme.

Supply (Chapter III). How much money is available in total for investment?

This problem has two parts. First, how much can be raised internally from depreciation plus retained earnings? Projections of the amount of cash that will be generated by the company's operations need to be supplemented by estimates of accumulated liquid assets, operating requirement for cash (liquidity preferences), and decisions as to how much will be paid out in dividends.

Second, how much will be obtained by outside financing? The first decision is whether any recourse at all will be had to outside sources. Many companies prefer to finance exclusively from depreciation plus plowed-back earnings. If money is to be raised outside, a choice must be made between debt and sale of new equity shares; and decisions must be made on the timing of borrowing or of stock issue as affected by conditions of the financial market and the timing of planned expenditures.

Rationing (Chapters IV to IX). How are available funds to be rationed among rival claimants whose requests usually exceed the supply of funds (in our example, $20 million requested, $14 million available)? The rationing process involves setting up standards of rate of return, sometimes differentiated for different kinds of investments, and appraising the composition of investments in the light of some general plan of company development. It raises questions of how the minimum rate of earnings required for any capital expenditure should be determined, whether different standards should be applied to different kinds of investment, how differences in risks among projects should be allowed for, and how to deal with projects for which no earnings rate can be computed or in which the strategic value exceeds measurable earnings attributable to the project.

Timing (Chapter X). How should capital expenditures fluctuate with changes in general business conditions? A company must balance the possible outlay savings that could come from depression investments against the added risks that imperfect foresight may produce obsolescence and excessive capacity and against the hazards of high cost of capital in depression financing.

PLANNING PERIOD

A major question to be faced before getting deep into the budgeting job is how far into the future the plan should go. Ideally, capital expenditures should be planned for a number of years ahead for several reasons. Long-term investments provide a framework for the future development of the company, which needs to be visualized in advance. Big economies of plant size, for example, may make it desirable to build capacity in anticipation of growth of demand (e.g., hydroelectric dams). There is usually a long gestation period between the time the project is planned and the time the plant goes into operation. Sources of capital usually require several months' advance planning also. Moreover, pronounced cyclical fluctuations occur in the amounts apparently needed (profitably investable) for capital expenditures. If any attempt is to be made to stabilize investment cyclically, long-term planning is needed. All these considerations underscore the desirability of projecting capital projects, at least in tentative terms, many years ahead.

Long-term capital investment programs that are integrated with company development plans are indeed not uncommon. In such cases, the capital expenditure budget starts with a comprehensive long-range plan for the company as a whole. Although the desirability of each individual capital expenditure should be tested by its prospective earnings, it must also be tested for consistency with this master plan. The probability that a given investment will produce the profits predicted depends in part on how it fits into the company's pattern of long-term development.[2] Capital expenditure plans of one of the building-material companies, for example, were derived from a ten-year development program. This master plan, made in 1935, started with a projection of the growth of sales of present products and the sales of planned additions to the product line and followed through marketing-methods plans and expected production costs to profits goals. The company then determined what capital expenditures would be

[2] Capital expenditures must also be paced with development of executives. Many companies had managerial indigestion after World War II. The men had not grown with the pace of planning projects, making plant additions, and putting them to work effectively. This restraint is emphasized in a study of capital budgeting practices of Minneapolis firms. (*The Minneapolis Project*, Investors Diversified Services, Inc., Minneapolis, 1950.)

needed to achieve this program and when.[3] Long-range plans of this general type became quite fashionable in the postwar planning orgy of the middle forties.

Dramatic and desirable though these brave dreams are, they exaggerate the precision with which a corporation can plan its capital life. The growth trend for established products in a growing industry can sometimes be projected ahead with precision, so that aggregate capacity that will be needed in some distant year can be foreseen.[4] But expansion of competitors and other factors that affect market share are hard to predict far ahead. Other kinds of capital expenditures are even more intractable. They are a little like prospecting: there is no telling what opportunities for profitable investment may be dug up by the company's own research or by dramatic technical advances in the equipment industry. Some companies which have tried five-year plans for capital budgeting have found that these projections are very tentative beyond two years. For all practical purposes, their capital budgeting is on an annual, or at most a two-year, basis, though they continue to look at the five-year budget and sometimes ask whether current projects were foreseen when the budget was drawn up. One of the large automobile companies, for example, estimates capital expenditure requirements two years ahead by quarters and revises estimates quarterly as a part of a complete operations

[3] Another company has a five-year budget for capital expenditures with these three components: a cash inflow forecast, including all internal sources of cash less dividends—annually for five years; a cash requirement budget, including both operating and capital outlays; an estimate of the outside money needed to fill gaps where it will be obtained. A major railroad thinks of its capital planning in terms of three periods: a 25-year stature goal, a five-year general facilities plan, and a one-year capital expenditure budget.

[4] A 25-year projection of the number of telephones in one of our large cities, made in 1925 by one of the telephone companies, proved correct within 5 percent, even though its predictions of growth during the thirties and of the general pattern of the location of the phones were inaccurate.

budget submitted by each division. There is an observed tendency to overestimate capital expenditures in the nearest two
quarters because projects take longer to get going than is
planned. There is, however, an offsetting tendency to under-
budget for the last part of the two-year period, because executives cannot think of all the things for which they need
money two years ahead. Thus the projection for the second
year is largely a pipe dream—but the best the division management can visualize as it peers into the future.[5]

In brief, explicit capital budgeting, as a practical matter, is
generally for only one year ahead. The projects envisioned in
longer-range capital planning are usually indefinite as to
amount, timing, and estimated profitability. These distant
projects, keyed to the company's long-range expansion program, are, so to speak, put on the shelf. Such projects may be
screened on the basis of rough estimates of their prospective
profitability, but there are limits on the precision that is worth
striving for in rate-of-return estimates of distant capital expenditure. Before they are put into the short-range capital
program, earnings are re-estimated more definitely.

LIMITATIONS OF APPROACH

The managerial problem of planning and control of capital
expenditure is examined from an economic standpoint. Ac-

[5] In reality this may apply as well to the one-year budget. McGraw-Hill found
in their 1950 survey of capital expenditure planning that 65 percent of their
sample companies review capital budgets monthly. There is thus much flexibility in budgeting over even the short run, and previously authorized projects
are continuously subject to the axe. (*Business Week*, January 21, 1950.) This
was borne out by flexibility of budgets in *The Minneapolis Project*. (See Footnote 2.) For a statistical comparison of planned and realized investment, see
Irwin Friend and Jean Bronfenbrenner, "Business Investment Programs and
Their Realization," *Survey of Current Business*, December, 1950, pp. 11–22.

cordingly, this discussion will be concerned primarily with principles and concepts and only incidentally with procedures and problems of organization for capital budgeting.

The capital budgeting process takes different forms in different industries. For example, in the automobile industry, where demand is growing, where product improvements and innovations dominate capital outlays, and where competitor's innovations continually peril a company's market position, neat rate-of-return rationing of capital is not common. Prevailing uncertainties dictate that the process of winnowing investment proposals take a different form, which is less formal but not necessarily less logical or thorough than the rate-of-return approach developed in this book. Executives do not think of a decision to develop a new engine as a rate-of-return problem. Instead, it is viewed as a many-sided decision of operating policy calling for collective wisdom in reconciling research dreams, production feasibility, competitive pressures, and market acceptance.

These qualitative considerations are usually focused on earnings, but often in terms of what is needed to preserve or enhance the earning power of the division as a whole, rather than incrementally in terms of how much added profits will come from the added investment. Thus, a car may be thought of as needing a new engine when its earning power (or market share) slips or is periled.

These various facets can be viewed as adding up to a rate-of-return estimate, but this economic structure is obscured by the heavy overlay of business judgment and grand strategy.

The theoretical and general aspects of capital budgeting are purposely emphasized in this book, which reflects the belief that the art of capital planning, that is, judgment on imponderables, can be best developed and exercised against the background of a formal economic analysis that has "gone about as far as it can go," and maybe farther. The most that can be usefully learned from any book is the generic and abstract skeleton of judgment. Putting flesh on the bones is the job of experience.

Chapter II

DEMAND FOR CAPITAL

A SYSTEMATIC SURVEY of the principles underlying the theory and measurement of a company's demand for capital expenditures is a necessary preface to the practical problems of capital budgeting discussed later on. This survey of demand for capital is followed in the next chapter by an examination of the supply of capital to the firm in terms of its principal sources of funds for capital expenditures.

SURVEY OF CAPITAL REQUIREMENTS

The usual starting point of a capital expenditure budget is a survey of the company's anticipated needs for capital. This inventory of internal investment opportunities is usually built up from the smallest operating units of the organization, often as an integral part of annual budgets or general development plans for a longer period. The catalogue of capital "needs," expressed in terms of specific individual assets, moves up through the management hierarchy for supervisory review and for aggregation into larger managerial units.

This capital requirements survey is sometimes guided by advance notice of the general state of supply of funds [1] or even

---

[1] For example, in one company the president sends out a letter each year to the divisional vice-presidents requesting each division to have its individual units submit tentative capital expenditure plans by a specific date. The letter sets the general background for that year's capital expenditures by presenting the

by specific "suggestions" on the minimum earnings rate that will be given serious consideration or the aggregate amount of funds likely to be available (e.g., each operating unit will be limited to 90 percent of its depreciation and depletion).

Behind the marshaling of investment proposals lie the discovery and creation of opportunities for capital expenditures. The backbone of a good capital budget is good projects—a surplus of opportunities to invest money internally at high rates of return, as compared with the amount of funds available. The worst that can happen from too many good opportunities is that the company may forego opportunities to invest profitably by not raising funds outside. On the other hand, a lack of good opportunities for internal investment may mean that a misallocation of economic resources will result from a policy of plowing back earnings without regard to profit outlook: there may be more profitable opportunities in other companies. The discovery and development of good investment proposals usually require effort. Hence encouragement of an imaginative search for such opportunities is an important part of the program. Since these opportunities stem from continuing efforts to find better ways of doing things, they come rather automatically as a product of good management. More specifically, the activities of the research department create these opportunities in new products, in improved products, and in advanced technology. Similarly, the industrial engineering group's efforts to find ways of reducing costs generally produce opportunities for profitable investment.[2] Good

president's views on the economic outlook and the supply of funds. In this connection he sometimes points out that building projects should be deferred because he thinks building costs are coming down or that, since the supply of funds is quite limited this year, all postponable items should be deferred. On some occasions he has set minimum payout standards in general terms for a category of investment for which payouts can be easily estimated.

[2] For example, a systematic survey of manufacturing operations in each plant

projects also result from research and competition in the equipment industries, whose business it is to promote their own sales by creating obsolescence.

Although long-range plans of company development are desirable, surveys of explicit capital requirements are, as noted in Chapter I, generally confined to one year or, at most, two years ahead. The capital projects themselves are hard to visualize in the distant future, since they depend upon unformulated technical advances and long-range development of demand for the company's product. And even when projects are foreseeable, their prospective earnings are highly uncertain, for they too depend upon unknown technical advances, market developments, and changes in relative prices.

NATURE OF DEMAND FOR CAPITAL

Surveys of capital requirements are often phrased in terms of "need." How much new capital will a given plant or marketing district "need" to do a good job (i.e., attain some kind of planned development) during the planning period? "Need" is a meaningless concept for economic analysis, since it contains no objective measurement of intensity. "Demand" for capital, in contrast, can be made meaningful, since it can measure the intensity of need for capital by its earnings. Under most circumstances, the underlying source of demand for capital expenditures is or should be prospective profitability.[3]

of a large electrical company was made by a team of industrial engineers and other specialists. As a result, projects were developed for mechanization and for altered plant outlay which promised high productivity of capital.

[3] This proposition is based upon the assumption that most firms try to make as much money as they can and that profits are their central objective. Our subsequent analysis of capital budgeting will take account of modifications of this profit-maximizing theory. For a discussion of profit policies, see Joel Dean, *Managerial Economics* (Prentice-Hall, 1951), Chapter I.

A company's investment proposals, when arrayed in a ladder of return on investment and when cumulated, form its demand schedule for capital. This schedule shows the total amount that is demanded (i.e., that can be invested) at any given rate of return.

The first step in projecting demand for investment funds within a company should be a survey of what investments may be needed to keep the company competitive and progressive. The next step is to appraise these projects by estimating the rate of return on each capital proposal. Then the demand schedule for capital can be conceived as the total amount of money that can be invested to earn more than specified rates.

DEMAND SCHEDULE FOR CAPITAL EXPENDITURES

To develop an empirical approximation of the company's demand schedule for capital for internal investment during a specified time period, it is necessary to marshal all individual "needs" for capital expenditures that can be discovered and foreseen throughout the company; to estimate for each proposal its prospective productivity in the form of rate of return on the added investment; to array projects in a ladder of rate of return (as illustrated by Table I); and to cumulate this ladder in the form of a schedule showing the amount of money that can be invested to equal or better each of a series of rates of return. Chart 2 diagrams the resulting capital demand schedule.[4]

---

[4] Often a project appears to be needed even though it promises a negative rate of return. This paradox is a sign that the computed return does not include the total benefits of the project to the company, usually because such benefits are intangible and hard to measure in dollars. Projects with unmeasurable returns cannot be fitted into the demand schedule, of course. Their treatment in the capital budget is discussed in Chapter IX.

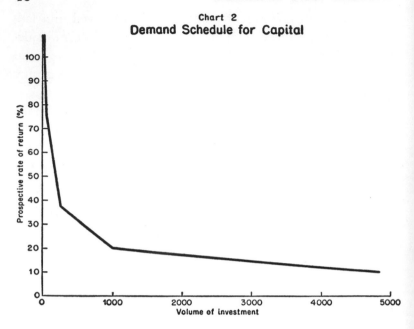

Chart 2
Demand Schedule for Capital

Table I

DEMAND SCHEDULE FOR CAPITAL

A	B	C
Prospective Rate of Return	*Volume of Proposed Investments*	*Cumulative Demand*
Over 100%	2	2
50–100%	38	40
25– 50%	200	240
15– 25%	1200	1440
5– 15%	3400	4840

In tabular form, the company's demand schedule shows the relationship between yield and cumulative totals of proposals; consequently it shows how much money can be invested at rates of return that will be better than a specified level. In drawing such a schedule, the time span must also be specified, and the assumption in Table I is that the common one-year capital planning period is used.

TIME DIMENSIONS OF DEMAND FOR CAPITAL

For simplicity, the firm's demand schedule has been conceived here as including only capital projects to be initiated during the budget year. That is to say, it includes only those investments whose productivity will never be higher than it is this year. Those that will get better if postponed should go into future budgets. Those that will deteriorate if postponed should be put into this year's demand curve. This simple conception concentrates on rivalry with alternative investments to be made this year. It ignores another dimension of rivalry, namely, with alternative investments that will be more profitable if made in subsequent years. To include future investments in this year's demand curve, it is necessary also to conceive of patterns for storing funds for later use. This storage can be in cash or in government bonds, or it can be in the form of investments that have high cash-to-cash turnover, even though comparatively low prospective profitability.[5] The cost of maintaining liquidity, to whatever degree, is an offset to the improvement in profitability of a later-year investment over a present-year investment. Rejecting a 20 percent return now to save money for a 40 percent return two years from now involves carrying costs. Conceiving of demand for funds with this time dimension, therefore, requires an exploration of the alternative time patterns of investment in terms of requisite liquidity. It ties the capital budget intimately into the long-run cash budget by

---

[5] Speculating on a fall in construction costs by getting along with temporary buildings is an illustration of this.

imposing dual standards, namely, productivity and cash payout.

Tax expectations also have a bearing on the timing of investments in projects where substantial parts of outlays are expensed against current income for tax purposes. When tax rates are rising, a deduction from future revenue reduces after-tax income less than a deduction from current revenue. Thus, if income tax is 40 percent this year and expected to be 60 percent next year, an asset that can be written off slowly by depreciation charges is cheaper than one that is totally written off against this year's income. This gives a differential productivity advantage to purchases of plant and equipment as against outlays for advertising or executive training. Conversely, when tax rates are high and expected to fall, advertising investments have a head start in productivity over outlays for tangible, durable assets.

PRINCIPLES OF MEASURING CAPITAL EARNINGS

The crucial estimate in analyzing demand for capital is the productivity (i.e., rate of return) of the proposed capital expenditure, and the care and precision with which capital productivity is estimated are likely to make the difference between good investment decisions and bad ones.

General principles for estimating capital productivity are summarized in this section. Application to different types of investment will be discussed in later chapters.

1. Recognition of the source of productivity of capital is essential to correct estimation of capital earnings. The source of earnings depends upon the nature of the investment. The most important direct sources are cost savings and sales expansion. Cost savings are the source for investments in replace-

ment and modernization of equipment. Added sales volume (or more profitable volume) is the source for investments that involve new products or expansion of capacity to produce old products. Earnings of many projects have more than one source.

2. Earnings must be estimated on an individual project basis. The prospective profitability of individual units of added capital investment is the key to their appraisal in allocating capital funds. Return on old, sunk investments has only historical interest and no relevance to decisions on new investments. And average return on old and new investments is badly misleading.

3. It is future profit on additional investment that is relevant. Thus, profit projections must be based on estimates of future prices, future costs, and so forth. The record of the past is useful only as a guide to estimates of the future.

4. Capital productivity estimates usually should involve comparison of future costs and profits with the appropriate alternative. An analysis of what will happen if no investment is made will reveal the proper alternative, that is, the least-cost method without added capital. Pains must be taken to make sure the comparison is with the relevant alternative, for the kind of cost comparisons that are valid will differ according to the nature of the alternative.

5. Capital productivity should usually be measured by earnings over the whole life of the asset, even though in practice the view of the distant future is often clouded up. Estimates of economic life (discussed further in Chapter VI) are always inexact, but they are essential for measuring capital wastage costs. Earnings may be stated in terms of the sum of gross earnings (or cost savings) over the whole life of the investment from which the cost of investment (i.e., capital

wastage) is deducted or in terms of net earnings, after annual allowances for capital wastage. In either case, the result is a rate of return on investment. For comparability, the company should standardize on one method. Payout period—that is, the number of years required for gross earnings (or cash savings) to pay back the capital investment—is a misleading measure of capital productivity. It is relevant solely for cash budgeting and then only when confined to cash earnings (or savings).

6. Discounting the stream of capital earnings to take account of the diminishing value of distant earnings is an integral part of the theory of capital value. It introduces complications of measurement, however. When the economic life of assets is short or fairly uniform, when earnings estimates are necessarily rough, and when uncertainty rises steeply in the distant future, this refinement is not worth its complexity cost. On the other hand, discounting has practical importance when there are distinctive time patterns of the income streams of different assets and when the rate of discount (logically the firm's cost of capital) is high, for example, 15 or 20 percent.

7. The amount of investment to be used for comparison with earnings should be the average capital tied up in the asset over the period affected by the decision. This period may not be the full economic life of the asset. Property whose final value, whether for sale or for other use inside the company, will be less than initial cost should be acquired only if gross earnings will cover this loss in value as well as the required return on capital. Determining how much of gross earnings represents capital payback rather than profits is a problem in financial mathematics, and the answer depends on the time pattern of earnings. In view of the manifold uncertainties of forecasting, the conventional straight-line depreciation account may fre-

quently be as good an estimate as any of capital payback.[6] In any case, the capital that has been liquidated by gross earnings is free to be invested elsewhere and is no longer dependent on the particular asset for its earnings. Thus some estimate of the average amount invested should be used, rather than the initial outlay.

8. Estimates of earnings (whether from cost savings or from added profits) should take account of the indirect effects of the proposed capital outlay upon the operation of existing facilities. Total company revenues and costs with the proposed investment should be compared with what they will be without it. Typically, estimates of these indirect earnings involve a high order of judgment and still have wide error margins.[7]

9. Estimates of the productivity of capital expenditures will differ in inherent riskiness and in the width of error margins. Some systematic method for allowing for these differences in risk and for comparing investment proposals is desirable.

10. When major changes in the price level are expected, the disparate changes of individual prices should be forecast as explicitly as possible in projecting both earnings and capital wastage (or appreciation). Differential timing of costs and revenues may have important effects on profits through price fluctuations. Changes in relative prices of capital goods and labor can substantially alter the productivity of an investment when technology and wages are both advancing steadily.

11. For some kinds of investments it is impractical to esti-

[6] However, when all the facts are known, the economic investment is usually seen to be different from the book investment. Accounting treatment, moreover, is properly governed by tax considerations and bookkeeping conventions, which have no bearing on investment decisions.

[7] When equipment that is displaced by new is pushed downward in a cascade of demotions (e.g., successive levels of stand-by or successive grades of service of locomotives or trucks), then the productivity of the new equipment includes the aggregate cost savings (or other earnings) of all retained equipment in their new uses.

mate a rate of return. The benefits are so diffused and conjectural (e.g., research laboratories and employee clubhouses) that they defy quantification. Earnings of others are so high and so apparent (e.g., replacing a washed-out railroad bridge) that estimating a return is an academic exercise. Earnings on other projects are patently too low to warrant return estimates. Capital productivity should be measured only when there is a factual foundation for estimates and for projects of borderline productivity.

Before developing these principles more fully in connection with their application to different kinds of capital expenditures, it is useful to discuss some controversial matters that have general applicability, namely, payout period versus profitability yield, postponability as an investment criterion, deterioration of capital productivity, and allowances for risk and uncertainty.

Payout Period versus Profitability Yield

Payout period is the time required to pay back the investment from gross earnings (with no allowance for capital wastage). It is a criterion commonly used in capital budgeting for appraising investment opportunities. It measures the rapidity with which the investment will replenish the capital fund. Payout period is essentially a cash concept, concerned solely with the cash budget and designed to answer the very specific question, "How soon will this cash outlay be returned to the firm's treasury?"

Of itself, the payout period does not measure profitability, in the sense of return on investment, and hence is not appropriate help in capital budgeting as contrasted with cash budgeting. For in limited-period investments, no fixed relationship exists between payout period and profitability.

Consider, for example, two alternative investment oppor-tunities to purchase cost-saving machines. Machine A costs $2,000 and will yield a gross cost saving (neglecting deprecia-tion on new equipment) of $500 a year for six years. Machine B also costs $2,000, but will yield a cost saving of $500 a year for ten years. For purposes of investment analysis, these estimated cost savings are properly regarded as estimated revenues. Thus, for both Machine A and Machine B, the pay-out period is four years:

$$\text{Payout period} = \frac{\$2,000}{\$500 \text{ per year}} = 4 \text{ years}$$

But at the end of the payout period, Machine A has only two more years of useful life, whereas Machine B will continue to yield annual revenues of $500 for six more years. Although their payout periods are equal, they are clearly not equally desirable investments.

The concept of profitability is concerned neither with cash budgeting nor with capital fund liquidity. Rather, it is con-cerned with the long-period maximization of income. Unlike the payout period, it does not focus on speed of paying off the investment; instead, it measures the income created over the entire life of the investment.

The rate of return on the investment refers in theory to the rate of interest that will make the present value of future gross earnings just equal to the cost of the machine. In the above illustration, the rate of return on Machine A is about 13 per cent, since this is the interest rate that discounts a six-year annuity of $500 down to a present cost of $2,000. Machine B has a 21 percent return, the rate that makes a ten-year annuity of $500 equal to $2,000 today. These calcula-tions are shown in Table II. The present-cost column on this table shows for each investment what the company pays today for \$500 income in the future; for example, when the money is spent on Machine A, \$500 in the fifth year costs \$272, but when spent on B, it costs only \$188. Clearly, B is a far more desirable expenditure, even though the two machines have the same payout period.[8]

Table II

RATE OF RETURN ON INVESTMENT

	MACHINE A			MACHINE B		
		Compound			Compound	
	Annual	Interest	Present Cost	Annual	Interest	Present Cost
Year	Income	Factor	of Income	Income	Factor	of Income
y	I	$(1.13)^y$	$I \div (1.13)^y$	I	$(1.21)^y$	$I \div (1.21)^y$
1	500	1.13	442	500	1.21	413
2	500	1.28	391	500	1.47	340
3	500	1.44	347	500	1.79	280
4	500	1.63	307	500	2.17	230
5	500	1.84	272	500	2.64	188
6	500	2.08	241	500	3.20	156
7				500	3.89	128
8				500	4.72	106
9				500	5.73	87
10				500	6.95	72

Total Present Cost			2,000			2,000
Rate of Return			13%			21%

Profitability yield, that is, the net return on investment, is the relevant criterion for developing a demand schedule for capital and for selection of projects. But in some situations payout period may be a valid subsidiary basis for ranking. When the firm's passion for cash is intense and it is unwilling (or

[8] This kind of computation, though enlightening, is much too awkward for common use. In practice, many kinds of approximation are made, with varying degrees of accuracy, that under the ever-present conditions of uncertainty are good enough. We cannot go into them in detail here, but in essence the correct ones all compare total expected income with cost and are not limited to finding the period required to get the cash outlay back. Differences are in the handling of the initial cost and in use of interest rates.

unable) to borrow even for short terms, an investment that speedily returns the cash may be preferred to one more profitable. In compromise situations, consideration must be given to speed of cash payback as well as to the underlying productivity of capital.

What explains the widespread use of payout period as a measure of profitability of capital outlays? To many it appears more simple, realistic, and safe than rate of return. It is somewhat simpler to compute, since capital wastage is not estimated. Ignoring these necessarily conjectural book costs confers on the payout method a halo of hard-boiled realism that appeals to some but is nevertheless a delusion. Payout, by weighting the near years heavily, has built-in conservatism, in facing the possibility that the earnings of the new machine may be soon destroyed by obsolescence. A short minimum payback standard, for example, two years, is one way of allowing for this uncertainty. But it does this captiously and crudely by counting only the earnings of the payout years. If it is clear that the cash will be returned before obsolescence or depression strikes, many companies are willing to take a gamble on profitability, which depends on what happens after the payout period. Rate of return, however, can be adjusted for uncertainty by methods that are more direct and flexible.

Postponability versus Productivity

Another widely used standard for choosing among investment proposals is postponability, that is, how long the project can be put off. If there is an excess of budget requests over available funds, many companies use postponability as a screen to reject projects that can be deferred, even though postponement would mean foregoing the profits made possible by an improved facility.

There is no necessary relation between postponability and profitability, although a spurious relationship appears for certain replacement projects. Postponing the replacement of a vital link (e.g., a pumping station on a pipeline) shuts down the whole operation. But the high urgency of this project stems from its terrific productivity, not from the perishability of the investment opportunity.

Selecting investments by postponability is not logical and is not likely to lead to allocation of investment that produces maximum profit. A large proportion of investments that would yield big savings and high profits could be put off almost indefinitely. For example, a service-station purchase, which would be lost to a competitior if not accepted this month, may earn only 6 percent, whereas a pipeline project, which could be postponed forever, would produce a 30 percent return in the form of cost savings. Under those circumstances the company would be better off to put its money into the more postponable, rather than the less postponable, of the alternate projects.

The use of postponability as a criterion is likely to result in a stagnant operation. The postponability standard would tend to forestall expansion investment and technological advance. To be sure, certain high-profitability items do happen to fall into the unpostponable class. But such projects are assured of acceptance through the comparison-of-profitability method, because the "must" items are high-profit items. "Must" items have high profitability automatically, because the alternative is catastrophe. For example, replacing a pumping station on a pipeline is enormously profitable, since, if it is not done, earnings of the whole line cease.

Deterioration of Capital Productivity

In a self-adjusting competitive economy, there is a tendency for capital expenditures to destroy the economic opportunity that creates their profitability. Abnormal profits are indicators of very rich opportunities for more investment, and expenditures will flow in their direction until increasing costs or output tend to cause firms to overshoot the optimum outlay level. In the process, they destroy the abnormal profits. This risk of destroying should be examined in connection with each profitability estimate.

A major source of earnings from captial expenditures is exploiting price disparities that are excessive under present costs. In the petroleum industry, this sort of disparity occurs among prices of different products and among prices of the same product at various market levels and locations. Thus investments in tanks in which to store heating oil in the Port of New York derive some of their profitability from the seasonal pattern of price spreads between the acquiring of heating oil near the bottom of the summer lull and either the acquiring price near the season peak or the higher incremental cost of producing heating oil at the seasonal peak when refineries must use more expensive processes. In early 1949 the price spread from summer to winter was more than a cent a gallon, whereas storage costs, including amortization of investment over a normal equipment lifetime, have been about three quarters of a cent per gallon. Such a price situation produces a profitable investment opportunity. But when seasonal storage capacity is built, distress prices at seasonal lows are bid up and seasonal peaks are shaved. Thus the investment devours the price spread that created its profitability.

Allowances for Uncertainty

A dollar of estimated revenue several years hence is worth less than a dollar today, not only because of the interest cost of capital, but also because of uncertainty about the accuracy of estimates. Future conditions may destroy all revenue from the investment. Technological advance may make the asset obsolete and worthless. Future changes in wages, costs, prices, and operating volume, may wipe out estimated revenues in future years.

Allowances for uncertainty are needed because risks are asymmetrical. It is possible that these economic changes will enhance profitability. But in a self-adjusting economy with a dynamic technology, it is more likely that they will reduce earnings. Moreover, management personally loses more from a bad venture than it gains from a good one.

Adjustments to allow for uncertainty may be challenged as being nothing more than guesses. Perhaps they are. But if so, they are guesses that must be made, and will be made, either explicitly or implicitly. Failing to apply the probability adjustments does not avoid the problem; it merely introduces the guess element in a disguised form at some other stage of the decision-making process.[9]

For the sake of objectivity, it is better to provide explicitly for uncertainty allowances in the capital budgeting methods. Allowances for uncertainty can be applied at various stages— while making the project's rate-of-return estimate itself; before the final budget review, by applying handicapping factors to the unmodified rate-of-return estimates; at the final review, by merely exercising general judgment without any attempt to modify the earnings estimates or by adjusting the rates of projects in some systematic way for differences in uncertainty.

There are several ways in which allowances for uncertainty can be incorporated into the rate-of-return estimate as they are being made. One way is to inflate the rate of discount, which normally allows only for cost of capital. Projects of

[9] When no modifications for uncertainty are incorporated in the earnings estimate, they may be taken into account in appraising investments—informally or by differential standards of acceptable rate of return.

different riskiness would then have different rates of discount, for example, 15 percent for a motor-truck replacement but 30 percent for a plastic moulding machine. Another way is to shorten the estimate of economic life of the asset to allow for the uncertainty of return on the investment. Uncertainty would be reflected by stepping up the expected rate of obsolescence, as in the five-year amortization of war facilities. A third method, which for some kinds of projects is more refined, is to apply a probability multiplier (e.g., .90, .85, .80 and so on) to the estimated earnings of each project for each year, where the multiplier is smaller for more distant years to reflect greater uncertainty. This method is capable of fine discrimination among years as well as among projects. It is particularly appropriate when the whole return from the investment becomes sharply more uncertain at some future date.

Thus, four different methods of allowing for differential uncertainty may be distinguished: informal judgment; application of differential handicaps to unmodified return estimates; modification of the estimate of life expectancy for uncertainty; modification of the estimate by probability multipliers applied to individual years.

The choice among these four methods depends upon the character of the uncertainty, and each of the four may be appropriate for particular kinds of investments. For example, if the existence rather than the amount of the estimated future revenues is uncertain, then the appropriate allowance is a probability multiplier which expresses the likelihood that the revenue in a particular year will occur. These uncertainty characteristics occur when there is rapid obsolescence of methods or of style, fickleness, and obscurity of forecasting buyers' tastes, particularly in development of new and unknown product lines.

ADMINISTRATIVE REQUIREMENTS

The method of applying these principles of measuring capital earnings will differ for different types of investment. Consequently, explicit application is discussed later for each main category. At this point three administrative requirements should be mentioned that apply to all categories of investment: the need for training in capital productivity measurement, the value of post-mortems, and the desirability of different stages of refinement in earnings estimates.

Training and Post-mortems

If these principles of measurement are to be adhered to and applied uniformly, training must be provided right down to the smallest administrative units. Moreover, systematic review of capital earnings estimates must be made not only by the immediate supervisor, but also by topside staff specialists. This review, particularly for large projects involving major expansions or entry into new product lines, involves a high order of experienced judgment, since all phases of the economic feasibility of the company's major development program come to focus when an estimate is made of the productivity of the capital.

Another administrative requirement is the post-mortem. The earnings rate actually realized on each capital expenditure should be compared with the earnings estimated at the time the commitment was made. This systematic check serves two purposes: estimates of capital productivity are taken more seriously when executives are held responsible for them; autopsies of estimating errors may improve techniques of guessing capital productivity.

Stages of Refinement in Estimates

Certain stages of top-management approval parallel the progress of a capital project from a long-range plan to eventual fulfillment. Three stages may be distinguished. First, the general plan is reviewed to see that it is consistent with a sensible general development program. Top-management concurrence in the long-range plan carries no commitment that funds will be made available. Next, definite projects are approved as components of the one-year capital budget. But budget approval is not an authorization to spend money. Lastly, funds are specifically authorized for individual projects.[10]

As capital projects pass through these stages of evolution from nebulous notions to definite requests for final authorization, different degrees of refinement in the measurement of return are appropriate. Three degrees of estimating refinement which parallel the three stages of approval might be instituted. First, back-of-envelope estimates are made roughly and rapidly by putting together already available knowledge. These estimates would merely feel out the economic feasibility and probe the survival chances of the project in a more rigorous capital productivity test. Next are the preliminary engineering estimates. These would be based upon considerable engineering analysis and rough forecasts of sales, prices, and other revenue factors. The estimates would be in terms of net return on capital and would be comprehensive enough to be submitted for the annual capital budget. Then come the final estimates. These would be the best projection of costs and revenues that

[10] Specific project authorization added to long-range plan approval and capital budget approval enables management to take another look at each proposal on the basis of the way the aggregate budget develops as the year progresses; that is, how much money is coming in, how the economic situation is developing, and at what rate capital expenditure is being made.

the divisional staff could make and would be reviewed and revised by a central financial staff and also by the capital expenditures group of top executives. Such estimates would be the basis for the final authorization to spend the money.

SUMMARY

The underlying requisite for effective capital expenditure planning is the opportunity to invest money internally at high rates of return. Such opportunities are in a sense a by-product of good management, but an imaginative search for them should be an integral part of capital budgeting.

A survey of the company's capital requirements built up from the roots of the smallest operating unit is usually the first step in capital budgeting. Ideally, capital expenditures should be planned for several years ahead as an integrated part of the company's long-term program. But projections become increasingly indefinite as they stretch into the future, and as a practical matter it is usually necessary to budget capital expenditures over a one-year, or at most a two-year, planning period.

The demand for funds for investment within a company can be viewed as a schedule of relationship between the amount invested and the prospective rate of return. To develop such a schedule, individual investment proposals showing estimated yield should be arrayed in a ladder of capital productivity summarized on a company-wide basis for a specified planning period. The demand schedule thus derived shifts with changes in general business conditions and with the fortunes of the firm.

To get good and comparable estimates of return on investment, the company's measurement methods must be built upon certain basic principles of measuring capital earnings.

The essential principle is that estimates should be based on the change in the company's total earnings and total costs that will result from the proposed investment. Only incremental effects are relevant, but all increments, including costs and revenues in other parts of the firm, must be brought into the estimate.

While payout period may have a bearing on some investment decisions, it is not relevant to all situations and should be subordinated to rate of return as a selection criterion. Postponability is an incorrect standard for deciding which projects to buy first.

In applying these principles, the detailed methods differ for different types of capital projects, but the probability that capital productivity will deteriorate, partly as a consequence of making the investment, partly as a consequence of technical and economic progress, should be taken into account. It is also important to have thorough education and good supervision in working out the detailed methods of applying these principles. Finally, different degrees of refinement in estimating the rate of return are appropriate at different stages in the development and review of a capital project.

Chapter III

SUPPLY OF CAPITAL

A COMPANY, in addition to exploring and measuring its demand for capital funds, must face the problems of determining where the money will come from and how much will be available.

A useful distinction can be made between internal and external sources of capital funds. The chief internal sources are depreciation charges and retained earnings.[1] External sources are principally sale of securities to insurance companies and to the public. (Term loans from financial institutions are not a source of permanent capital, since they must be paid off by either retained earnings or later security financing. They are a means for postponing the financing problem.) In the internal disposition of these funds no distinction should be made on the basis of sources of funds. In particular, the internal investment process should deal with gross rather than with net business savings—that is, with income before allowance for recovery of plant costs. In so doing, a desirable fluidity of the internal investment process is achieved. Old, dying products can subsidize the capital formation required for launching new ones by making contributions to the company's capital funds that are not "earned" according to a "net" income concept. Consequently, internal capital formation becomes more flexi-

---

[1] In the short run there are secondary internal sources such as sale of property or reductions in working capital that represent liquidation of existing assets. An analysis of policy for disposal of assets is discussed in the Appendix.

ble than external financing. The distinction in conventional accounting between replacement reserves and net income is a restriction on inter-company flow of capital that is not present in inter-product flows of capital within one company. The practice of allowing each of a company's divisions or plants to reinvest its own depreciation charges without central-office review carries division autonomy too far and undermines a major social and private advantage of multiple-product firms. Cash earnings, rather than net earnings, should be pooled in a centrally administered supply of capital.

INTERNAL SOURCES

The principal managerial problems in connection with internal sources are to forecast how much cash will be generated internally and to decide how much cash to pay out in dividends.[2]

In modern corporate enterprise, capital expenditures are usually derived from internal sources. In some companies, capital expenditures are confined completely to the amount that can be obtained internally. This may be a matter of choice or, in some sense, a matter of necessity in the light of the condition of the capital markets or the investment status of the firm. (In *The Minneapolis Project*, cited in Footnote 2 of Chapter I, it was emphasized that virtually every company interviewed made *realized* profits a prerequisite for capital expenditures. This finding is contrary to the economist's notion that *expected* profits from the expenditure are the necessary condition and that past profits are irrelevant). Consequently,

[2] What proportion of the retained funds should be made available for capital expenditure as opposed to use in regular operations and reserves for emergencies is a problem of allocation of capital. Hence it is a problem of demand, not of supply of capital.

the projection of the amount that can be expected from accumulated depreciation and retained earnings is usually the most important part of capital expenditure budgeting. Some companies make elaborate five-year forecasts of the cash that will be generated and of its disposition for dividends and for liquid reserves. More commonly, such estimates are confined to a one-year or two-year period. Such projections are not only a matter of forecasting the level of sales prices and costs; they also involve management decisions on the adequacy of depreciation charges, the level of dividends, and the necessary degree of liquidity.

Depreciation

The purposes of depreciation and depletion charges are so various that no one method can fulfill them all. One managerial purpose is to hold back funds for replacing the asset. Depreciation charges based on prewar costs are inadequate for replacement at the postwar price plateau. If pricing and dividend policies are based on inadequate charges, the company runs the risk of inadvertently losing money in terms of economic reality or paying dividends that are not really earned. This hazard may be removed directly by depreciating on a replacement cost basis. The choice between historical cost and replacement cost is the important economic decision for depreciation accounting.[3]

The hazard may be met indirectly by setting up price level adjustment reserves or bigger contingency reserves or by issuing niggardly dividends, making much of the *de facto* depreciation reserve look like surplus on the balance sheet. The accounting

[3] In comparison with this decision, the choice of straight-line, sinking fund, or annuity methods and so forth is unimportant in the light of the vast uncertainties in guessing service life and future price fluctuations.

form of allowance for price level change is immaterial; the important thing is that an adequate allowance be made.

Occasionally, depreciation and depletion are used as criteria for the allocation of the capital budget among units in the company. It was, for example, fairly common during the great depression to confine each major operating unit to a capital budget that was no more than its depreciation and depletion of some fraction thereof. In some instances this practice was carried down to regional marketing investments and to individual plants. Use of this criterion for allocation of capital funds among small units shows a blind faith in the *status quo*. Such a faith has little justification, particularly in periods of adversity.

Retained Earnings

A second internal source of capital funds is retained earnings.[4] The amount from this source depends not only on the amount of earnings, but also on dividend policy and plowback policy. The proportion of earnings that is retained varies greatly among firms and from year to year and generally has a pronounced cyclical pattern. The stability of dividends compared with earnings has several explanations. Managerial tenure is strengthened by paying some dividends through the thick and thin of business cycles out of retained earnings of prior years if necessary. Dividend continuity is an important factor in the cost of capital. Investment opportunities are generally richer when earnings are high than they are in de-

---

[4] The major role of retained earnings in capital formation is easily shown by a little arithmetic. Over a period of 15 years, a company earning 15 percent on equity capital can triple its net worth by plow-backs even while paying out half of its earnings in dividends. There are numerous spectacular illustrations of this achievement in industry, such as the Chrysler Corporation, which increased the book value of its stock eight-fold by plow-backs in the 22 years from 1925 to 1947.

pression and justify retention of a larger part of income. (See Chapter IV.) The extraordinarily large proportion of earnings plowed back during the postwar boom reflected this second factor plus the recognized inadequacy of conventional depreciation charges for replacing equipment at postwar price levels.

Plow-back guides. The importance of retained earnings as a source of capital funds makes plow-back policy an integral part of a firm's capital expenditure budgeting. How should a company decide how much of its earnings to plow back and how much to pay out?

One guide to plow-back policy is that outlined by the capital rationing theory set forth in Chapter IV. If a company follows this plan faithfully, it retains earnings (up to the limit of stockholder rebellion) as long as they can be invested at a return higher than the firm's cost of capital (e.g., 15 percent). It pays out earnings that cannot be invested internally (either now or in the future) to beat this cost-of-capital rate.[5]

Another guide is suggested by the theory that dividends in the modern corporation are a kind of interest income (although more uncertain than contractual interest). If plow-back policy is determined by this theory, then retained earnings would be a highly volatile residual left over after paying stable dividends out of fluctuation earnings.[6]

[5] The stockholders' opportunity cost is not always well measured by the company's cost of capital. The underlying assumption of this analysis is that the stock market's appraisal of risks and prospects is reasonably accurate so that the market value of its stock is on a par with other stocks when risks, fluctuations, and so forth are taken into consideration. When this assumption is incorrect, the cost of capital to a particular company is not a good measure of the stockholders' foregone opportunities.

[6] Stockholders' reactions to plow-back policy differ according to their income-tax brackets. Rich stockholders may prefer heavy plow-backs (if they earn good returns), which can be taken as capital gains, to big dividends that are taxed at high marginal rates. Higher dividends are preferred by low-income stockholders and investment organizations whose performance is judged by the yield of the

A third guide to plow-back policy is found in the notion that a certain percentage of earnings should be held back for contingencies and for growth. This is a long-run view of an average minimum amount of plow-back that would rate a prior claim on earnings over an integral business cycle.[7]

Plow-back and cost of capital. The effects of plow-back policy upon the market price of the company's stock, and thus upon the firm's cost of capital, may modify these three approaches. There is some evidence to support the hypothesis that plowing back (as opposed to paying out) earnings depresses the price of a stock and thus raises cost of capital, at least temporarily. Additional evidence is provided by the fact that the securities market has on the average and over the long run substantially discounted the value of retained earnings. Alfred Cowles II found that for the period 1871–1935 total retained earnings of a large group of companies were 35 percent of their income. Market price increases over the 65-year period reflected only 72 percent of the company growth from these undistributed profits.[8] That is, on the average, the market was willing to pay only 72 cents for a dollar of plowed-back earnings. Thus there is some evidence that high plow-backs depress the stock's price and thus raise the cost of capital.[9]

---

stocks they buy. When the company wants to sell new stock, the latter groups probably hold the balance of power in setting the offering price. When new stock is not in the question, the direct pressure of stockholders on management probably lies with the high-income investors, in so far as there is pressure. If holdings are widely scattered, management's plow-back freedom is assured by stockholder inertia and by management's control of the proxy machinery.

[7] This consideration in plow-back policy is an allowance for uncertainty. Strictly, cash is one kind of capital investment and thus an alternative use of plowed-back funds. But it is not usually thought of in this way. Hence, this factor of added liquidity as part of plow-back policy deals with uncertainty by non-rationing criteria.

[8] Cowles and others, *Common-Stock Indexes* (The Principia Press, Inc., Bloomington, Ind., 1939), pp. 43–44.

[9] Possibly this interaction of dividend policy and cost of capital is a phenomenon of a short time-span that tends to wash out over a longer period. Companies

It is logical to expect that from the standpoint of the effect of plow-backs upon market price and cost of capital there is an optimum ratio of retained earnings. Paying all earnings out in dividends connotes impoverished opportunities for internal investment, no plans for growth, and inadequate contingency reserves. On the other hand, plowing back too much generally depressed stock values, as perhaps indicated by the Cowles study. The levels of these limits vary among companies and depend upon the prospects for profitable growth and the type of investor that holds the stock. Market-wise, small new companies have much to gain by plow-backs, since their stocks are typically held for a speculative capital gain. Large companies with widely held stock tend to assume a social responsibility for dividend stability to maintain consumer income for the widow-and-orphan class of investor.[10] Since large companies, moreover, have much easier access to capital markets than do small ones, they have less need for a policy of high retained earnings for growth.

EXTERNAL SOURCES

Historically, the capital markets have not been as large a source of investment funds as the internal sources have. During the twenties and again in the four-year period 1946–1949, net new security issues supplied about 25 percent of new corporate capital and gross corporate saving supplied 75 percent.[11] In the thirties, with demand for capital unusually low,

---

that plow back heavily in an early development period (e.g., Johnson & Johnson) have a high cost of capital then, but may get a lower than average cost of capital at a subsequent time when dividends are stepped up.

10 AT&T provides an example of rigidity with its $9.00 dividend, which has been maintained since 1922. This rigidity has given the stock much of the character of a high-yield bond, and there is a widespread attitude in the company, the market, and regulating commisssions that to cut it now would amount almost to a default on interest payments. But commisssions tend to view the $9.00 as also a solid ceiling to allowable earnings.

11 The statistical materials underlying this conclusion are weak and only roughly

capital issues fell to 18 percent of their level in the twenties,[12] and there appeared to be a trend in corporate financing toward greater self-sufficiency in supplying capital out of savings. This trend was disturbing to many observers, who felt that the market's social function of allocating capital resources was being atrophied. But whatever the merits of the argument, the problem of excessive plow-backs is older than the big depression.

Role of Cost of Capital

When a company considers using outside sources to finance investment, a basic factor is the cost of capital, which for common stock is the ratio of prospective earnings per share to the selling price for new shares. By comparing the company's cost of capital with the prospective profits of new investments, the gain to present stockholders to be derived from going after outside funds can be measured. Theoretically, there is no point in going outside unless present equity stands to gain. If a project promising a 25 percent return is financed by sale of new shares to investors asking a 20 percent return, the number of outstanding shares will be increased less percentage-wise than total earnings, and per-share earnings on existing shares will increase. But if the return appears to be 15 percent, the number of shares increases more than total earnings, and per-share earnings fall.

In theory, the cost of capital plays another role. It shows the return that could be made by diverting cash out of the

---

relevant. They have more than the usual number of gaps and non-comparabilities and do not justify detailed description. Complete statements of source and use of funds for non-financial corporations are available for the postwar period only, and these are not totally reliable. For the earlier period, the picture is sketchy and obscured by investment trusts and holding companies.

An important study on this question is Irwin Friend, "Business Financing in the Postwar Period," *Survey of Current Business*, March, 1948, pp. 10–16.

[12] Stock issues were 35 percent of total issues in the twenties and 22 percent of total issues in the thirties. Based on data published periodically in *Commercial and Financial Chronicle*.

firm's business into alternative market investments. That is, it is the opportunity cost of retained earnings. Tax leakages blunt this measurement if capital is withdrawn in the form of dividends, which are taxable as stockholders' income. To dodge the tax leak, it is possible to have a partial liquidation, which may be taxable only as a capital gain, or to have the company itself invest in securities of other companies, which postpones the tax question indefinitely. This opportunity-cost principle has a tone of unreality, however, since it implies that the stockholder is king and that financial policy is aimed solely at maximizing the value of his capital. In most companies profit maximization in the financial sense is qualified and transformed to allow for management's own ambitions to grow or for their natural desires to avoid the capital markets and the SEC. As a result, cost of capital is seldom used as a signal for retaining and distributing capital.

For outside financing, on the other hand, cost of capital has much practical importance, at least in the negative decision not to invest when profit prospects are less than cost of capital. But, as will be seen, it does not always act positively to stimulate investments with profitability above the market rate. From a conceptual viewpoint, however, cost of capital is an important guide to capital budgeting, and its level should be known.

Determination of Company's Cost of Capital

A company's cost of capital fluctuates with the company's fortunes and the condition of the security markets. It differs greatly among industries and companies. Nevertheless, the cost of capital can be estimated with sufficient accuracy to make it a useful capital budgeting tool if the foregoing philosophy of its role is accepted. As a practical problem, estimating cost of capital has three elements, finding market values, finding costs of flotation, and determining capital structure.

At some point, a decision must be made on the time period involved in the estimate. The choice lies among a long-run average of past years, a projection of long-term future costs, current spot cost, computed continuously (or annually at capital budget time), and spot cost at the time flotation is contemplated. These four possibilities usually give significantly different results.

In principle, the decision on where to cut off capital expenditures and when to supplement internal funds from external sources should be governed by current cost of capital.

A serious drawback to this rule is the fact that cost of capital fluctuates violently and that stockholders have long memories and slight comprehension of these matters. Selling stock in bear markets to take advantage of internal investment opportunities that are rich (in relation to self-generated funds) apparently makes existing stockholders unhappy. Many, who are unable or unwilling to exercise rights, have the "birthright for pottage" illusion. Conversely, raising equity funds at the top of a market leaves a bad taste when the market sinks. Some managements consequently try to hit the middle range, preferring to borrow temporarily or forego profitable investments in order to promote illogical stockholder happiness. Expected long-run future cost appears more practical from this standpoint. The best index of the future is usually an average past cost of capital.

Market Values

The first step in finding the company's cost of capital is to estimate for the relevant time period the market value of debt and equity securities of the type that the company plans to use. This is not a simple problem. Market prices of the company's own securities may be *prima facie* evidence of short-run costs, but it is difficult with a sample of one to eliminate all the non-recurring factors (e.g., shifts in management or product line) that qualify current belief about the particular company's earning prospects. Estimates based on several companies with comparable risks can improve reliability. But the sample must be carefully selected to insure that it is homogeneous in the important long-run elements that determine market price.

Cost of debt capital raises few important problems, since bond prices depend on a fairly narrow range of factors and are dominated by the government bond markets. The use of debt capital varies widely among industries and is perhaps to some extent influenced by custom. Manufacturing corporations have traditionally had a relatively small amount of funded debt in their capital structures. After the war, interest costs of all corporations were about 8 percent of income before taxes and interest.[13]

Clearly, estimates of debt cost can be made highly precise in comparison to the uncertainties of estimating costs of equity capital, and when debt and equity are combined to find the total cost of capital, errors in interest cost estimates are negligible.[14] More important may be the effect of the presence

[13] Irwin Friend, "Business Financing in the Postwar Period," *Survey of Current Business*, March, 1948, p. 15.

[14] However, there appears to be a trend toward an increased use of debt for marginal external financing. (See Starhle Edmunds, "Financing Capital Formation," *Harvard Business Review*, January, 1950, p. 36.) Such a practice may substantially increase the reliability of capital cost estimates. Several factors have combined to give a bias toward debt financing. The most important of these factors are the increased flow of capital through insurance companies, who are limited to debt securities in their investment portfolios; the convenience of placing an issue privately with such institutions, as compared with going through the SEC machinery; and the relatively high risks (and thus costs) of floating new

of debt on cost of equity capital. (See "Capital Structure" below.)

The cost of equity capital presents more formidable estimating problems, concerning both the prices of securities and the costs of flotation, which are substantially higher than costs of floating debt capital. The basic difficulty stems from the nature of equity capital and the forces that set its prices. "Cost of equity capital" has a double meaning. From management's viewpoint, it is the relation between management's estimate of prospective earnings and current prices, which are set by the mysterious and volatile forces of the market place. From the investor's viewpoint, it is the rate of discount he applies to his own estimate of future earnings, and it is thus a measure of his uncertainty. Current prices fluctuate not only with changes in the market estimate of future earnings, but with the current degree of uncertainty as well.

Either of these concepts involves more speculation about the future than does the cost of debt capital, and both depend on some factors that have no statistical gauge. Any estimate of the cost of equity capital based on statistical analysis thus relies on broad assumptions as to the relevance of measurable current and historical data in estimating the market's expectations.

The most universally used measure of the cost of equity capital is the ratio of current prices to current earnings, which would seem to be irrelevant from either management's or the market's viewpoint. Its implication about investor sophistica-

---

common stock. One method of debt financing, popular recently, is to sell real estate to insurance companies and universities and then to lease it back. This arrangement amounts to a debt contract with a sinking-fund provision. By such devices, a company is able to liquidate a relatively low-return investment and reinvest the funds in high-return production facilities. This form of debt has an unjustifiable superiority from the standpoint of balance-sheet appearance, since by conventional practice such rent obligations are only footnotes to the balance sheet, whereas bonded debt is written up at the capital value of the liability.

tion—namely, that the market expects current conditions to continue indefinitely—is hard to accept.

Nevertheless, statistical analysis shows surprisingly close relations of prices to current earnings, provided that dividends and perhaps book values are also brought into the picture by multiple correlation analysis. Although such analysis is empirical and hence has no objective index of market expectations, it provides a useful benchmark in forecasting the price at which stock can be sold in terms of expected earnings and dividends at the time of flotation.

Estimates of cost of capital can frequently be made more economically by following market behavior directly than by analysis of such apparently controlling factors as growth trends, sales volatility, and so forth. Thus, for an established company whose stock is well known and heavily traded the practical problem is to forecast the condition of the general market at the time the new issue is to be floated. Such a projection often is sufficient for capital budgeting, provided it is based on recent market performance, since the new issue will not alert the stock's investment character. For companies whose stock has no active market or no market at all, market value may be estimated by statistical analysis of comparable companies. For instance, the combined experience in price-earnings ratios of a large sample of companies of roughly similar size and similar products (e.g., groups as large as durable producer goods or processed foods) over the cycle gives some background information on long-run capital costs. Price-earnings behavior for a few highly similar companies may also be a good first approximation if the market's attitude on these few is well understood. Some investment bankers start from this point in the search for a "right" offering price on a new issue.

Costs of Flotation

The cost of capital in terms of trading prices for outstanding bonds and shares is only the first step in estimating the marginal cost of capital. The relevant figure for the company is the net proceeds from floating new securities in the market. These proceeds depend on the costs and inducements of security flotation, which are of three types: underpricing, that is, the spread between the normal market price and the offering price required to dispose of a block of new shares; commission and discount to underwriters as compensation for services in marketing the securities; flotation expenses incurred by the issuing corporation in connection with the sale.

Underpricing is necessary to allow for the possibility that a decline in the general market will undermine the success of the offering. An additional allowance must be made for the depressing effect on the market price of the particular stock caused by the offer itself. Such market response is almost always experienced; it comes partly from the selling pressure of those who cannot exercise rights. It also comes from doubts about whether the new money can immediately be put to as profitable use as the old. The size of this underpricing allowance depends on how great a chance management wants to take that the rights will become valueless and the issue unsuccessful because of general market decline and pressure of the offer.

Compensation to underwriters in the form of commission and discount varies greatly, depending upon the kind of company and the size of the issue. The corporation's cost of flotation, the third element, also varies with the size of the issue and, for large issues, is a trivial percentage.

Estimates of these three adjustments can be made with fair accuracy from an analysis of market price behavior and from a study of SEC data on past costs of flotation. For extreme differences in size of flotation, there are marked differences in aggregate costs of flotation that affect cost of capital. However, costs are flat over a wide range of size of issue. This range encompasses the range of choice of most companies that have practical access to the public securities markets.

Capital Structure

A company's cost of capital depends not only on the cost of debt capital and the cost of equity capital; it also depends on how much of each kind of capital it obtains. The debt ratio has a simple impact on combined cost of capital because debt is much cheaper than equity capital. Nowadays, debt capital costs about 3 percent, while equity capital costs 10 percent or better in terms of current earnings. Clearly, a capital structure of two-thirds debt, which is characteristic of some electrical utilities, will be cheaper than a structure with no debt at all, which is found in many manufacturing companies.

But the capital structure itself affects the cost of equity capital. A high debt ratio (in relation to the volatility of earnings) not only increases the dangers of default on debt, but also heightens the risks of common-stock ownership, and thus raises the cost of equity capital. This interrelationship makes the composition of the minimum cost package a matter for technical advice, particularly since it changes with conditions of the security market.

A third factor relating capital structure to capital cost is the corporation income tax, which makes the unjustifiable distinction between interest as a deductible expense and dividends as taxable earnings. If the government takes, say, 50 percent of earnings (after deducting interest expense), investments financed with stock must have gross (before-tax) profit prospects that are twice as high as debt-financed earnings in order to yield the investor a comparable return. Thus the over-all cost of capital in terms of earnings before tax depends on the mixture of non-taxable and taxable earnings. For example, assume that both bonds and stocks sell to yield the investor 5 percent earnings and that the tax rate is 50 percent. A $1,000 investment financed entirely by debt need earn only $50; if half of it comes from equity capital, it must earn $75; and if it is wholly financed by stock, it must be able to earn $100 to get the $1,000 from the market initially.

In principle, it is the prospective cost of additional permanent capital that is relevant for most capital budgeting problems. But here, as in pricing problems, it is important to distinguish between short-run and long-run incremental costs. Clearly, the cost of a credit line at the bank is not, for long-term capital projects, an appropriate concept of incremental cost of permanent capital.

Thus, since there is a considerable range of managerial discretion in balancing the added risks of more debt against its cheaper costs, the capital structure constitutes another dimension of management choice in determining the firm's cost of capital.

COST OF CAPITAL FUNCTIONS

The foregoing analysis indicates that a company's cost of capital is the function of several variables, many of which are to a degree within the control of its management. Among these are plow-back policy, capital structure, level of the market at the time of issue, kind of issue, amount of funds sought, and market fame of the company. The company's cost of capital has a wide band of managerial discretion, the width of which depends partly on the degree to which these variables are stabilized by the company's history.

These variables (plus others) affect the level of a company's cost of capital function. Many of them also affect its shape—that is, where it turns up as the amount of investment increases. As indicated previously, it is probable that the cost of capital function is flat over a wide range of investment. But at some point it rises, and probably precipitously.[15] (See Chart 3.) The point of upturn moves right and left with stock market conditions, even if the horizontal segment of the curve remains fixed.

Where this point is depends on the market conception of the ability of the company to put the added funds to profitable use. This conception shifts with the condition of the security markets and incorporates a large element of faith in the ability of management. Although large, established firms may be unaware of the rising phase of their supply curve, it is easy to find examples of firms which have experienced this abrupt limit on the amount the "market will absorb."

Perhaps the most important determinant of the average future cost of capital that is within the control of management is the timing of equity (and debt) flotation. The giant fluctuations of market prices create opportunities to keep the cost of outside capital low by picking the right time. Manipulating dividends and making short-term bank loans make it possible to ride through periods of high capital cost and to

---

[15] Basically, the point of rising cost ought to depend on the market's appraisal of the firm's opportunities for profitable growth and its ability to exploit them. Retained earnings may indicate, in good times, management's confidence and may thus influence outsiders' appraisal of these profit opportunities. But in other periods, earnings are retained because of fear for the future, to increase the firm's liquidity.

maintain a dividend policy that is optimum from the stand-point of cost of permanent capital. These practices also open opportunities to finance this year's outlays with future years' retained earnings and bring into focus the problem of time-rivalry in the supply of funds. There are, as we have seen, severe limitations on how far it is politic to go in speculative timing to minimize the company's cost of capital.

In private placements (i.e., sale to one institution or to a few institutions) a different mechanism operates. Typically, an insurance company offers to take $10 million in 3 percent bonds and perhaps another $5 million in a 4 percent bond with rigid safety precautions. It will take no more under any circumstances. Here the supply curve, instead of rising continuously with size of flotation, has only one step and is vertical at $15 million.

These concepts of the cost of capital function will be directly applied in the examination of capital rationing theory in Chapter IV. But first a digression will be made to examine the aversion to external financing and the economic consequences of autonomous capital formation.

AVERSION TO EXTERNAL FINANCING

This whole problem of the cost of external capital is a matter of no concern to many companies, simply because they have no intention of ever using outside funds.[16] For many firms it is a source of pride that they never go to the market for financ-

16 In McGraw-Hill's "1950 Survey of Capital Spending Plans," the companies were asked, "Would you boost 1950 spending if you could sell new common stock for 50 percent more than its present market price?" Only 7 percent of the companies said Yes. There were a number of reasons for this response, but it is a significant indication of the demand for equity capital, in view of the fact that a price increase of this magnitude would carry the Dow-Jones index 70 points higher than it had ever been, except during the 1929 boom. (*Business Week,* January 21, 1950.)

ing a new opportunity, no matter how profitable it appears. They determine the amount of capital available for new schemes not on the basis of earning prospects, but on the basis of availability of cash from retained earnings above the balance needed to meet the ironclad standards for the current ratio.[17]

Reasons for Aversion

What are the reasons for this aversion to debt and this demand for liquidity among modern business managers? [18]

First, debt financing for venture purposes cramps management's style. Most bank loans and bonds carry restrictions on the uses to be made of money, on future financing, on minimum levels of certain balance-sheet items, and on dividend payments. They further put a fixed capital cost on the firm, since a periodic cash outlay sometimes extends into the unknown future, regardless of conditions or opportunities. Preferred stock, though legally different, is not as a practical matter much better in this respect. Furthermore, debt lowers the credit standing of the firm and smears the balance-sheet façade that is such a large part of management's reputation. This fact gives added attraction to getting capital by leasing assets instead of purchasing them, since in leaseholds neither the asset nor the liability is shown on the balance sheet. It would be in-

[17] A sample statement: "It is traditional with Sun Oil Co. that capital funds for purposes of expansion must come from internal sources. In this, we have followed a conservative practice, for we have permitted growth to take place only as fast as our company developed the internal ability to provide the means of growth. As a consequence, we believe that our company has maintained its characteristic qualities of independence and self-reliance, making it a stronger competitor in the oil industry and a more stable member of the business community than it would otherwise have been." Statement of Robert Dunlop, President, Sun Oil Company (80th Congress, 2d Session, 1949, Report of Joint Committee on the Economic Report on Profit Hearings, p. 104).

[18] The possibility of a formal theory of the firm's liquidity preference is discussed by W. W. Cooper, "Revisions to the Theory of the Firm," *American Economic Review*, December, 1949, pp. 1204–22.

teresting to see the balance sheet of the A&P or Safeway stores, with all their lease liabilities written up.

Second, debt financing puts an asymmetrical risk on management. The men who make the decisions rarely regard the profit prospects as adequate to offset the threat offered to their personal security by general reorganization in bankruptcy. In many corporations, management's share in the profits of successful ventures (in the form of dividends on the stock they own) is an insignificant source of income compared with their salaries, which show admirable stability over the business cycle. Dividends are marginal income for management and are subject to steep marginal income tax rates.[19]

Executive bonuses based on profits help to balance this asymmetry, but do not cure it entirely. The profit bonuses of the individual executive are often not the result of initiating the slowly ripening profitable venture. Instead, they are the result of being there at the right phase of the cycle. Thus, despite stock-ownership and profit bonuses the personal interests of executives are usually toward conservatism. Who is to condemn (or even know) if management turns down a

[19] This point was brought out in some empirical studies made during the thirties. R. A. Gordon found that in a sample of 161 executives the median holding of stock in their own company in 1935 was $298,000 and the median dividends were $2,980, while median total compensation was $79,200.(*Business Leadership in the Large Corporation*, Brookings Institution, Washington, D.C., 1945, p. 298.) The SEC found the following picture of management holdings of securities in their own companies for the 200 largest non-financial corporations (*TNEC Monograph*, No. 29 [1940], p. 60):

	Mean Holding	Median	Management Holdings as a Percent of Total Value of All Issues
Officers	$ 50,400	$ 9,300	0.1%
Officer-Directors	763,400	33,400	1.9
Directors	753,100	21,000	3.5
All (Officers and Directors)	$616,000	$20,000	5.5%

risky venture that might cost them their jobs if it miscarries? [20]

In the modern large corporation, equity financing of expansion (sale of new common shares) is free from debt restrictions and usually also from threats to control. With ownership widely scattered and passive and with management in control of the proxy voting machinery, there is rarely a significant protest from stockholders about the uses that are made of their capital. On new offerings of common shares, stockholders are usually given rights to purchase their proportionate shares at the offering price, and this price can usually be set low enough to make rights valuable to them. For major expansions, equity financing thus provides a reasonably safe source of new capital (from management's point of view) for large corporations, even though SEC regulations now make security flotation a costly and time-consuming operation.[21]

But even new common stock is not without its perils to young and fast-growing industries, where the need for new capital is greatest. In marketing a new and speculative security for a small company, it is never clear what the right price is and who the large buyers will be. In the early days of the electric power industry, General Electric and Westinghouse undertook to provide capital markets for the securities of the new and specu-

[20] To be sure, a well-publicized coup can produce substantial gains on the market value of executives' stock (subject to the much lower capital gains tax rate), but such capital gains only create a pressure for short-run maximization of apparent profit prospects when executives want to sell stock. The importance of such manipulations for the sake of the insiders' capital gains has been greatly diminished by the SEC's new regulatory powers over management's stock transactions.

[21] In the light of management's apparently impregnable position in equity financing, the reluctance of corporations to sell common stock in the bearish postwar markets is a mystery. The fact that stocks were being traded at prices far below management's estimate of their value in terms of profit prospects somehow made it seem "wrong" to sell new stock in such a market. Desire to maintain an established dividend rate could explain the aversion, if management doubted that the net proceeds of the cheap stock could be invested profitably enough to cover the dividend comfortably.

lative utility companies, since the utilities were the principal market for electrical equipment. As a consequence, however, the small utilities soon found themselves buried in the holding-company structures that proved to be the most expedient method for the manufacturers to sell to the public and to recover their own cash.[22] Similarly, AT&T had an office revolution in 1907 when it was bailed out of an unsuccessful offer of convertible bonds by the Morgan-Baker banking interests. Wherever the company is small and risky relative to its sources of capital, voting control remains a delicate and precious wand that must be guarded carefully, even at the expense of potential growth rate.

The private consequences of a policy against outside financing will be examined in the next chapter. For a company with this kind of policy, the cost of capital has in practice little usefulness, except when internal investment prospects are extremely low compared with other parts of the economy. A street railway company, for instance, may generate much more cash through depreciation charges than it can invest at a rate of return as high as that which an oil well promises. In the private interests of the stockholders, the best use of the money is probably a distribution to stockholders for investment elsewhere.

Social View of Autonomous Capital Formation

A serious criticism of autonomous capital formation by big business is that corporation management thereby evades an objective market test of the desirability of the capital expenditures as compared with all other uses of funds.

Profits have a dual role in capital formation. First, their re-

[22] Westinghouse itself had to go through the reorganization wringer in 1907, when utility financing undercut its working capital, even though it was basically a sound, going concern.

investment provides funds for capital formation. Second, the prospects of profits entice new money into the kind of economic activity that needs it, as judged by the criterion of demand and supply. If competition were fully effective and if profits were not the result of basic changes in the price level and the inadequacies of historical accounting, then profits would exist only when and where they were needed to induce capital formation. Profits are "exorbitant" when supply is inadequate to meet demand, and high profits entice new investment and lead to heavy plow-backs by existing firms in order to keep their market share. The resulting expansion of capacity tends to correct the supply deficiency. Prices come down, and exceptional profits disappear, having performed their salutary economic function.[23]

Ideally, if a corporation paid out all its earnings in dividends and then went to the capital markets for funds that it needed for internal investment, the flow of economic resources would be directed to the kinds of capital formation most needed, where "need" is measured by prospective profitability. When large corporations refuse this market test by retaining their earnings, there is at least the possibility that capital will go to the wrong places. Management's allocation of capital expenditure may be distorted as compared with the market's impartial allocation; sectors of the economy that need capital will suffer because sectors that have capital want to grow.

The allocation of capital inside a well-managed, giant corporation may compensate by its efficiency for the lack of an impersonal capital market test of the desirability of its internal investments. The rationing of capital inside such a company is likely to be cheaper, easier, and more expert than the

---

[23] The term "profits" has many meanings. It is used here in the sense of a residual earnings left after paying all costs, including interest on owners' capital and wages for owners' time devoted to business.

rationing among companies performed by the capital market. Within the confines of the company's area of know-how, a good system of capital expenditure budgeting and control can perform the economic function of directing capital to its most profitable use (and presumably, therefore, to its highest economic service). Probably the job is done better than could reasonably be expected if all funds were paid out in dividends (and chipped by the personal income tax) and then returned to the company by having each product division bid for funds against all other companies in the capital market, instead of merely against all other divisions within the same corporation.

When the capital expenditure proposals go beyond the firm's area of specialization, the superiority of internal rationing is more dubious. Moreover, when the marginal rate of return departs seriously from the company's external cost of capital, efficiency in rationing within the corporation cannot compensate for blocking the flow of funds throughout the economy by quasi-automatic regulators of profitability.[24]

SUMMARY

A company's chief internal sources of supply of funds for capital expenditures are depreciation reserves and retained net profits. No distinction between these two should be made in the apportionment of internal investment.

The chief managerial problems in respect to internal sources are forecasting the amount of cash that will be generated and

[24] Scattered returns indicate a great disparity in the prospective rates of return of the least profitable investments made by different corporations in different industries. Presumably this disparity indicates that distortion of resource allocation may be taking place. In defense of retained earnings, it should be recognized that the capital markets are not as perfect as envisaged by this theory and that high personal income taxes cause substantial leakage to the Federal Treasury when earnings are paid out in dividends.

deciding how much earnings to pay in dividends and how much to plow back in capital expenditures.

Dramatic changes in price level throw doubt on the replacement adequacy of depreciation allowances based on historical cost. Extracurricular allowances and outright increases in plow-back are needed to assure replacement.

Retained earnings are a major source of capital funds. Plowback policy is affected by many considerations, such as opportunities for investment inside the company as opposed to outside, regularity of stockholders' income, reserves for contingencies and growth, and the effect of plow-back on cost of capital from outside. Dividend policy frequently becomes an autonomous determinant of internal capital supply, through company traditions of paying out a fixed percent of earnings each year. In such cases, dividend policy may be *the* strategic factor in capital expenditure budgeting.

The pivotal consideration in external supply of funds is the cost of capital. It should signal dividend payouts that restrict internal supply and also indicate when and how much recourse should be had to external supply.

Estimation of cost of capital involves determination of market values of securities, cost of flotation, and capital structure. Cost of capital is affected by many factors over which management has some control—company policy on plowbacks, capital structure, the level of the market at time of issue, size of issue, amount raised, and market fame of company. Projections of future costs of capital, therefore, have a wide band of control, its width depending partly on the stabilization of these variables by company policy.

Management's aversion to external financing, which is quite common, stems from distaste for possible restrictions and fear of upsetting the established organization. It cuts off a large reservoir of means for exploiting opportunities and puts narrow limits on sources of capital supply.

Autonomous capital formation raises questions of broad economic policy which have an important practical bearing upon the pattern of business investment plow-back. The undoubted efficiency with which some big companies apportion funds within the fold may more than compensate for the fact that individual operating units do not have to meet the market test for funds. But it cannot be relied upon to overcome the injury to our resource allocation system when the corporation as a whole invests money internally at prospective rates of return that depart significantly from its external long-run cost of capital.

Chapter IV

CAPITAL RATIONING

CHAPTER II explored the company's demand for capital by translating an inventory of capital expenditure "needs" into a demand schedule for capital. It is also sketched how this schedule could be approximated empirically by making an estimate of the capital productivity of each project and by arraying these estimates in a priority ladder of prospective rate of return. Chapter III examined the supply of funds to a firm for capital expenditures. The principal sources of funds were surveyed, and some of the considerations were indicated that affect the amount to be obtained from each source. Finally, the theoretical relationship of the supply of capital to its price was sketched. Demand and supply can now be put together as a conceptual basis for appraising individual capital expenditure proposals in what may be called a theory of capital rationing.[1]

The purpose of this chapter is to sketch a theory of capital budgeting in the sense of an ideal, though practically unattainable, plan. It is stated categorically and in abstract terms and requires an unreal precision in foresight and estimates of

[1] Any system for rationing resources requires a criterion for comparing recipients. Normally, prices and incomes are the basis for rationing goods, although in war additional criteria of "war needs" are set up for scarce and critical materials. The theory of capital rationing proposed here compares projects in terms of rate of return in contrast to methods of capital budgeting that use no systematic acceptance tests. Qualifications of the theory, however, make up a major part of this book.

capital productivity. For simplicity, it abstracts from important practical problems that will be discussed later.

REJECTION RATES

Practical rationing requires not only a ranking of projects according to a ladder of profitability, but also a rejection standard to separate projects that are not sufficiently profitable to merit funds from those that are. Theoretically, this cut-off rate of return is automatically determined by the intersection of the demand and supply curves. Thus, how much to invest and what the cut-off rate should be are two sides of the same coin. This relationship is logically correct under the assumption of our theory, but in practice, cut-off rates are set by management.

The rejection rate has three uses in administrative control of capital budgeting. The first is to provide a tentative forecast of return expectancies for a next-year budgeting program. In this form, the rejection rate embodies a forecast of an uncertain and unknown demand schedule and a projected internal supply schedule. Such forecasts of the rejection rate are necessary to top planning because time-lags and imperfect foresight make it impractical to wait until the relative profitability of individual projects has been determined and until the resulting schedule has been compared with supply as determined by retainable earnings and cost of capital. Rough as it is, the resulting rejection rate provides some basis for immediate decisions on dividends, financing, and minor capital projects.

The second use of the rejection rate is to weed out projects that have too low a profitability to justify further attention at either divisional or top-management levels. It is thus a tool for economizing executive time.

The third use is to implement a long-run capital budgeting plan that seeks to avoid making marginal investments of low productivity in times of slack investment demand. Funds thus preserved can be invested for higher returns when demand turns up again.[2] In this form, the rejection rate is a rough substitute for budgeting that includes the rivalry of proposals to be made at different dates. (This method was sketched in Chapter II.) It requires, however, a projection for an integral business cycle of both the total demand curve and the total internal supply curve. Making this projection is worth while only when the firm's capital sources for the cycle as a whole are so inadequate when compared with demand that the long-run cut-off point is far above the cost of capital.

Conceptually, four forms of rejection rate of return can be distinguished: a fluctuating effective rate of return that may move up and down with phases of the cycle or with conditions of the treasury and that will determine the cut-off point for normal projects at any one time; a basic minimum rate of earnings that sets a normal floor for any projects in any phase of the cycle; a stable long-run rate that is frozen as *the* cut-off rate for all phases of the business cycle; exception rates of return that differ for different kinds of investment to accommodate disparities in risks and the needs of grand strategy. Some circumstances may justify sheltering certain kinds of investment from the full rigors of competition with all alternative uses of capital funds on the basis of capital productivity.

The effective rate and the minimum rate can be used as a team for short-term budgeting. The long-term rate is an alternative to this team; it is a different system used for coping with cyclical fluctuations. Exception rates can be used in con-

---

[2] For example, the cut-off rate for expenditures in all phases of the business cycle might be stabilized regardless of short-run shifts in demand and supply.

nection with either of these two types of rationing schemes, since such rates may take the form of handicapping differentials.

FLUCTUATING EFFECTIVE RATE

The fluctuating effective rate of return is, in our theory, located at the intersection of the forecasted demand and supply curves for capital, but the rate at any time is set at management's discretion as a means of regulating and timing the amount of capital expenditures. A major oil company, for example, has varied the effective rate from a five-year crude payout in the depths of depression to a one-year payout during the postwar boom. Another company, which has a perennial minimum standard of 15 percent, has at times raised the effective rate to as high as 50 percent.

The underlying reasons for moving the effective rate up and down include variations in the supply of funds available to the company for capital expenditure; speculations on price changes for capital equipment; fear of general declines in business, which produce a high liquidity preference; and informal deflation of earnings rate estimates.[3] (These reasons for cyclical instability of capital formation are discussed in Chapter X.)

The fluctuations of the effective rate may in part be caused by a desire to hoard funds in anticipation of future demand

[3] During boom periods, anticipations concerning future earnings tend to become inflated, despite Herculean efforts topside to keep middle management's feet on the ground across the business cycle. Some companies have informally deflated these oversanguine boom-time earnings prospects by raising the effective rate. For example, one oil company has taken the position that declines in the price level of petroleum products will convert an apparent one-year payout proposal into a two-year payout proposal. Hence, the effective rate should be high when petroleum prices are high.

for capital more favorable than today's demand. Better profit prospects may come in the future from price changes, from improved productivity of specific projects that ripen with the passage of time, or from general economic changes that increase opportunities for capital investment. As will be pointed out later, manipulation of the effective rate is not a precise instrument for coping with inter-temporal rivalry of projects whose productivity improves if postponed, since it cannot deal with them on an individual project basis.

In formulating the theory of the effective cut-off rate, two situations need to be distinguished—the autonomous firm that is determined to limit itself to internally generated funds only and the company that is willing to go outside for additional capital funds, either occasionally or regularly. The distinctive nature of the budgeting problem in these two cases stems from the shape and behavior of the supply curves.

Autonomous Financing

Panel A of Chart 3 diagrams the situation for the company that is limited to plow-back earnings for its supply of capital. The demand schedule D_1 portrays for each prospective rate of return the amount of money that the firm can invest internally for earnings of at least that rate. Point P on the curve, for example, shows that this firm can invest $10 million at a rate of return of 20 percent or better during the planning period. The shaded area indicates that there is a wide area of uncertainty about this demand function and that the function is in a sense the most probable value in this error band. A smooth demand function is a simplifying extremity that abstracts from the fact that capital proposals are lumpy and discrete, usually causing the firm's statistical counterpart to descend in steps.

The curve D_2 is the demand function in conditions when

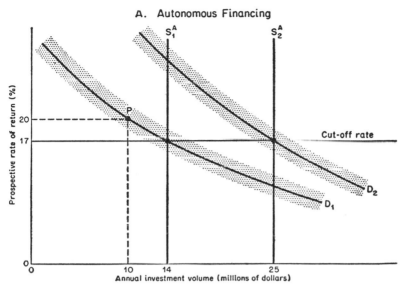

Chart 3
Fluctuating Effective Cut-Off Rate

A. Autonomous Financing

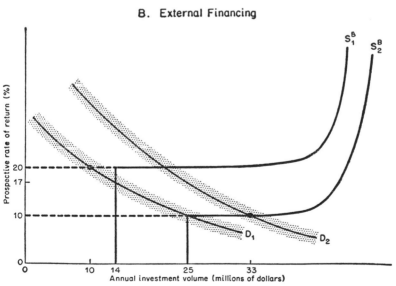

B. External Financing

"needs" for capital expenditures are extremely pressing and profitable, such as in the period immediately following World War II.

The supply curve corresponding to D_1 is the vertical line, S_1^A. Drawing it as a vertical line emphasizes that, as a practical matter, many companies' internal supply of funds seems to be unrelated to other opportunities for using the money. In Chapter III it was noted that to maximize profits for stockholders some measure of the cost of outside capital should be used as a floor for fluctuations in the cut-off rate. The effect of this rule is that when demand is so slack that marginal prospects are already down to the cost of capital a further fall in demand produces a horizontal shift to the left in the supply curve. That is, the rule signals higher dividends and lower retained earnings.[4]

Viewing the business cycle as a whole, how does the cut-off rate for autonomous firms behave? For reasons discussed in Chapter X, shifts in the demand curve are likely to be accompanied by parallel shifts in the supply curve, since the volume of investment prospects is related to current income. This parallelism tends to reduce the fluctuations in the cut-off rate, as illustrated by the boom-time curves S_2^A and D_2 in Chart 3, where, to illustrate the point by extremes, no change at all is shown. It is clear from the diagram that, in general, nothing specific can be said about the relative level of the cut-off rate in boom and prosperity, since this level depends on the relative swing in the supply and demand curves. When supply fluctuates more than demand, cut-off rates will be higher in depression than in prosperity.[5]

---

[4] This conjectural interrelationship is most easily viewed as a horizontal shifting of the supply curve rather than as a sloping supply curve, which would imply a high correlation between cost of capital, demand for capital, and the amount of retainable earnings.

[5] A case can reasonably be made that high cut-offs in depression are the usual

When demand is so slack that the cut-off rate limps along at the cost of capital (and this situation is conceivable in either high or low business activity), its fluctuations depend, of course, on conditions in the capital markets.

Although this theory portrays a company that under no circumstances is willing to use outside money, in practice a cut-off rate that goes much above the costs of capital will act powerfully to undercut this policy and induce the company to engage in some temporary borrowing. How high this rate needs to be to send the company to the banks is a matter of surmise, but it is hard for a company with a 10 percent cost of capital to reject a 50 percent rate of return that must be externally financed.

External Financing

For a company that is willing to use outside money, Panel B of Chart 3 illustrates the determination of the cut-off rate. In contrast to the autonomous supply case, the whole supply function discussed in Chapter III is relevant here. As illustrated by S_2^B, it extends to the right from the limit of retainable earnings to the point where the market says, "Enough!"

Here, again, depression-shifts of the demand curve to the left that are drastic enough to cause a cut-off rate less than the cost

---

situation. Management's interests point toward stabilizing dividends and maintaining them, at least nominally, through depression. Dividend stability increases the volatility of the supply curve, particularly when, in deficit years dividends are paid out of past earnings. But since demand for capital in depression is for cost-saving devices, industries with slow technical progress may have wide swings in the demand curve as well.

Whether the cut-off rate is higher or lower in boom than in depression may also depend on the nature of the boom. The postwar boom rested on a demand for capital goods that had accumulated through a long depression and war. Thus the demand curve was exceptionally high and tended to boost the cut-off rate. With equipment shortages *per se* eliminated, demand shifts downward and reflects only routine replacement needs. Receding backlogs of demand lower the cut-off rate of earnings as such a boom progresses, provided the supply curve is maintained far to the right.

of capital call for an increased dividend payout, rather than for the use of funds for submarginal expenditures. Thus, the demand schedule D_1 meets the supply schedule S_1^B at a 17 percent cut-off, while the cost of capital during the period is 20 percent. In this case, the company should ideally pay an extra $4 million in dividends and reduce their planned plow-backs from $14 million to $10 million. As the demand curve shifts to the right, the cut-off rate will remain substantially horizontal to much higher levels of expenditure than most companies recently have been willing to venture. (That is, the supply of money seems to be much too elastic to raise the cost of capital in the relevant range of demand.) The whole supply curve may also shift cyclically. Just how it shifts is a matter of speculation, but, in general, something like S_2^B, illustrated in Panel B of Chart 3, might be expected in prosperity. The relation of D_2 to the new cost of capital, 10 percent, indicates that the company should raise $33 million of new capital, $8 million more than the $25 million planned from plowed-back earnings. Not only are the retainable earnings usually smaller in depression, but the securities market's estimate of prospects is gloomy enough to raise the cost of capital substantially.

A company's cost of capital should, according to this theory, call the signals that regulate supply of funds. When cost of capital is low (e.g., 10 percent) as compared with the rate of return (adjusted for risk) on marginal internal investments (e.g., 15 percent), then outside financing is indicated. When the least profitable investment that can be made from cash generated internally is below opportunity cost of capital, generous dividends are signaled. Thus cost of capital signals when dividends should restrict internal supply and when and how much recourse should be had to external supply.

BASIC MINIMUM RATE

An important adjunct to the fluctuating effective cut-off rate is a basic minimum rate below which the effective rate shall not go, no matter how much internal supply exceeds demand for capital. Its purpose is to keep the company from making investments that cannot earn enough to pay their cost of capital. Hence, this minimum rate should be set by anticipating future cost of capital. If the company is in a position to manipulate its short-term financing so as to raise permanent capital at low-cost times, then this floor rate will usually be lower than current, or even a long-period average, cost of capital.

But many companies do not know their cost of capital, and when no outside financing is in prospect, management may not see the relevance of capital markets to budgeting. Nevertheless, when such companies use supply-demand rationing of funds for capital budgeting, they recognize the need for some minimum return standard and understand fully that it is wrong to plow back earnings to the point where marginal profitability is zero.[6] When the cost of capital is eschewed, the minimum rate can be set by various standards such as the following.

The company's long-term average rate of earnings on past investment is sometimes used. This minimum is sometimes justified by reasoning that it represents an earnings rate with which stockholders have been satisfied in the past and that it is

[6] The minimum argument for a cut-off rate is that earnings prospects should not be less than the discount factor for uncertainty that reflects the probability of out-of-pocket loss on the investment. (Uncertainty discount factors are discussed in Chapter II.)

functionally effective in an economic sense, since it seems to compensate for the risks of the enterprise and to have attracted capital needed for growth. Setting the minimum rate higher than this average would result in a refusal of investments earning rates that have in the past satisfied stockholders. It would probably also result in slowing down the rate of company growth as compared with what it would be if past earnings were the standard.

This kind of autonomous historical standard is, from the viewpoint of the economic system, unsatisfactory, unless it happens to coincide with the company's long-term cost of capital. If the average earnings rate is lower, capital is retained when it could be put to more productive use elsewhere. If the resulting minimum is higher than the firm's cost of capital, the firm invests at a slower rate than the vast impersonal forces of the capital market would cause if outside capital were sought in order to make the rejected submarginal investments.

Sometimes a company goal rate becomes the minimum standard. Some companies have a clear-cut notion of an adequate rate of earnings for the company as a whole. This rate is determined in part by the opportunity to make more than this and by strategic limitations imposed by considerations of public and political and labor relations.[7]

THE LONG-RUN CUT-OFF RATE

The third major kind of rejection rate is the long-run rate that cuts across the cyclical swings in earnings prospects and is based on tentative guesses of demand and supply of funds in

[7] For example, one large company reported that its minimum rate-of-return standard of 30 percent before taxes (at standard volume output) was its goal rate of return on net investment. This goal rate was evolved over the years as a "reasonable rate of return"; its origins are historic and rather indefinite.

a five-year or ten-year budget. The purpose of this kind of cut-off rate is to avoid having to pass up high-profit projects in times of high demand because funds were squandered on low-return investments in times of low demand. The long-run rate is different from the basic minimum rate in both purpose and level. The basic minimum serves largely as insurance against major boners in investment, whereas the long-run rate tries to put the next ten years' investment opportunities on a single demand curve to compete for the ten-year supply of funds.[8]

The long-run rate is not a logically complete approach to long-run capital budgeting. Investments made this year do not necessarily compete with investments to be made four years hence for the supply of funds, particularly if this year's investments have a high cash payout rate. In its pure form, a long-run plan is a sequence of outlays and corresponding revenues that extends to the forecasting horizon. Alternative plans embody different kinds of equipment or different dates for purchasing the equipment, and the best plan is the one with the greatest present value. For instance, one plan might be to set up a system of regional warehouses this year, when materials are available but markets still undeveloped, with a prospective 30 percent return. An alternative might be to establish markets first and postpone warehouse outlays for three years, after which they would show a 40 percent return unless costs had

[8] Our discussion of demand for capital has shown how difficult such projection is. With dynamic technology it is hard to foresee what kinds of opportunities may occur years hence, to say nothing of knowing how much money they will cost and what the return will be. Although five-year forecasts of the cash-generating ability have been made, they depend for their accuracy upon projections of national economic activity over heroic distances into the future. The cost of capital from outside can be guessed for the long-term future on the basis of an average in the past only by assuming that the capricious stock market will follow historical patterns in the future. Thus the empirical foundation for this kind of theoretical solution is frail.

risen. The funds could meanwhile be invested in projects with fast payouts—perhaps advertising—or even in liquid form such as marketable securities.

Obviously, the long-run cut-off rate cannot include this time dimension of competition for capital—that is, the same project at alternative dates. No project can enter the long-run demand curve more than once, presumably at the rate of return that corresponds to optimum timing of the expenditure. This demand curve therefore implies that a single plan has already been determined as the best and that the long-run cut-off rate reflects previous planning decisions.

The long-run rate, therefore, cannot be the single tool for capital budgeting, since the rate is itself dependent on the decisions about the really big projects. Nevertheless, it often has much administrative value. Long-run planning in terms of alternative investment schedules, such as those mentioned above, must usually be limited to budgeting for the few grand schemes that dominate company ambitions. Planning for smaller projects becomes lost in uncertainty as the planning period is extended. The alternatives are too numerous and interrelated to be plotted out in detail. It is here that the long-run cut-off rate can be brought into use, in the routine budgeting of these lesser proposals. If management has established a broad view of the company's future, the long-run rate can be made a time-saving device for tying the minor parts into an integrated scheme.

EXCEPTION RATES

The fourth kind of rejection rate is the special rate that includes a handicap allowance to give strategic investments a head start in the race for capital funds. For example, petroleum companies commonly have a concept of "balanced" investment in production, refining, transportation, and marketing capacities that overrides profitability criteria on individual projects. A goal of eventually achieving production of 75 percent of the crude that is marketed may be achieved by assigning to well-drilling investments lower cut-off rates than to service stations. Similarly, territories where coverage is inadequate or where earnings are below standard may get handicap rates.

Actually, of course, an exception rate is a confession of ignorance—the intangible benefits of such strategic investments are unmeasurable in dollars. The handicap allowance is a guess at the inadequacy of the profit estimate and, being a guess, has little rational foundation. (Determining the level of exception rates is discussed in more detail in Chapter IX.)

ASSUMPTIONS OF THEORY

Any economic theory is necessarily based on a set of simplifying assumptions. The theory of capital rationing presented in this chapter makes the following assumptions.

1. It assumes, as usual in economic theory, that the objective of the enterprise is to maximize profits in a narrow and calculable sense of the word. But narrow profit maximization is not the only, or, in fact, the usual, goal of large corporate enterprise.

2. It assumes perfect foresight of all the opportunities for investing capital inside the company. Only by making such an assumption is it possible to conceive of a definitive demand schedule for capital expenditures, and only by anticipating

future capital requirements is it possible to engage in the process of comparing investment opportunities that are inherent in the concept of capital expenditure budgeting. No company can hope to attain the assumed omniscience in anticipating its capital expenditure needs.[9]

3. It assumes that the prospective rate of return on each capital proposal can be projected with precision. Accurate forecasts must be made of the amount of investment as well as of the added profits from the added capital outlay. Only by assuming the measurability of capital productivity is it possible to set up a framework of economic analysis for this problem.

4. It assumes that the risks of all projects either are equal or have been accurately reduced to uniformity by a handicapping system that adjusts the rate of return for the proposal to a level that makes risks equal. Obviously, inherent hazards and the range of error in estimating both return and risk differ greatly among proposals.

5. It assumes that the firm has access to the capital markets for raising equity money and debt money and that the rates for each can be ascertained, so that, given a debt ratio, the combined cost of capital is determinate both currently and over the long run. Companies differ greatly in their *de facto* access to securities markets. The markets are themselves quite imperfect, and cost of capital is for many enterprises hard to determine (e.g., those whose securities are not listed).

The emphasis of the theory, furthermore, is on what may be a more special case than the author thinks—namely, a situation in which the opportunities for profitable internal invest-

[9] It is a common experience for distant plans to understate subsequent capital expenditures, because executives cannot visualize all that will be needed. Conversely, near-term budgets tend to overstate actual expenditures, partly because of purchasing delays, but partly because the plan is padded with all contingent expenditures. This is discussed more fully in Chapter I.

ment exceed the supply of funds that the company is able or willing to devote to capital expenditures.

The justification for using such a conceptual model is that it provides a simplified framework for subsequent analysis by showing what must be estimated, how, in general, estimates can be made, and how the results of the estimates can be logically fitted together. But it is only a starting point, since the theory overstates the degree to which capital budgeting can and should be mechanistic. Such formal systems will not take the place of good business judgment, but may channel and refine that judgment.

This capital rationing theory has greatest applicability to the middle-size range of investments. It is not controlling in making large pivotal investments. These large investments are so important that they command protracted study from various viewpoints by top executives. The high command has more faith in its own judgment than in the comprehensiveness and accuracy of rate-of-return estimates made by staff people. On the other hand, it is not worthwhile to apply so elaborate a system to relatively small investments.

The coverage of this theory is incomplete in another way. The theory is dubiously applicable to investments where foresight is very imperfect, error margins are big, and strategy bulks large. It is wholly inapplicable to investments for which no rate of return can be estimated.[10]

10 Clearly, some kinds of investments cannot come into bare-knuckled rate-of-return rivalry, simply because their rate of return cannot be measured. Investments in research laboratories must be made largely on faith. Employee welfare investments such as cafeterias and washroom facilities also have an indeterminate productivity. Other kinds of investments may be held out because tests other than the rate-of-return test appear more appropriate. Some companies, for example, exclude replacement investments (e.g., a motor vehicle fleet) from any capital productivity standards and, instead, use a routine replacement time schedule developed by rules-of-thumb experience.

ALTERNATIVES TO RATE-OF-RETURN RATIONING

The approach to capital rationing sketched in this section is valid in principle, and though limited in applicability, it serves as a standard of reference for appraising other methods of capital budgeting. Some of the alternative attacks are considered in this section.

A common method, which is the antithesis of a rate-of-return system, is to let the determination of the total amount of capital expenditure and its allocation among projects be governed solely by the judgment of top executives who "consider each project on its merits" and tailor the total as best they can to the company's purse. This intuitive approach, when applied in large companies, burdens top management with a multitude of decisions that must be made without objective criteria. Hence, the appraisal of an investment proposal is influenced by top management's appraisal of the executive who proposes it and by his persuasiveness in presenting it.

A similar approach, which is characteristic of public utilities, is to appraise projects not on the basis of prospective individual profitability, but on the basis of what is needed to provide adequate service. A return standard for the individual project is presumably not necessary because demand is inelastic enough so that future price adjustments will provide an adequate return for used and useful investment. Thus, rate of return neither governs the total nor guides its apportionment among projects.

Another method widely used in industry is to size up individual investment proposals against an ideal of company balance and growth goals. For example, in the petroleum industry, a company might seek, as a long-run objective, a 50 percent growth in a decade and the attainment at the end of ten years of crude-oil production and refining facilities that equal its marketing demand. Such a goal may provide a criterion for approving and rejecting investment proposals. Whether it will be a more satisfactory criterion than the rate-of-return rationing plan outlined above is doubtful. The effects of this kind of plan upon the company's long-run rate of return are difficult to determine, because this approach views the company as a monolithic strategic investment. "Balance" usually means some form of vertical integration, and vertical integration has not proved universally profitable in all industrics, nor is it sure to reduce the hazards of the enterprise.

Another device is postponability screening. Sometimes both the total amount and the allocation among individual projects are determined by whether or not the proposed investment can be put off.[11] (An appraisal of postponability is found in Chapter II.)

SUMMARY

Capital rationing is central in the planning and control of capital expenditures, since requests for funds normally exceed supply. Screening proposals on the basis of their prospective rate of return (when measurable) puts capital rationing on an economically sound foundation and limits the degree to

[11] A New York lawyer innocent of any experience with feathered chickens bought a rundown chicken farm in southern New Jersey and hired a local farmer to run it. Every two months he toured his domain with the farmer, who invariably pointed out needs for capital expenditures—new chicken coops, fences, and so on. The lawyer's invariable reply to the first request for a project was, "Money is scarce; you will just have to fix it up and make do." The second time the project came up, the reply was the same. If a project was requested a third time, it was granted. This was the criterion of capital rationing evolved by the lawyer to protect him from his ignorance.

which persistence and persuasiveness can influence the allocation of funds.

The essence of the capital rationing theory is to find the rate of return at the point where the demand curve from Chapter II and the supply curve from Chapter III intersect. All proposals with a higher prospective yield are carried through, and all that are less promising are rejected. The intersection rate of return—that is, the cut-off—is the pivot of the proposed capital budgeting procedure, since it is the administrative criterion for accepting or rejecting candidate proposals. Theoretically, this cut-off rate is determined exogenously, but in practice rejection rates are, for administrative reasons, set by management using rough forecasts of the intersection rate. The cut-off rate serves to kill off unworthy projects at the roots of the organization and to help deal with rivalry of funds among time periods.

Four kinds of rejection rates can be differentiated: the fluctuating effective rate; the minimum rate, which is stable and serves as a floor for the effective rate; the long-run rate, which is alternative to the plan that combines effective and minimum rates; and the exception rates, which serve as differential handicaps for categories of investment that require unusual rejection standards because of differences in measurability or risks.

The effective rate fluctuates with projections of the rate at which demand and supply curves will intersect. It is also manipulated for the purpose of regulating the firm's rate of investment to deal with temporary dearth of funds, speculation on changes in prices, anticipation of deterioration in the general economic situation, and informal deflation of the rosiness of boom-time estimates of capital productivity.

The minimum rate of return should be set on the basis of a projection of the future average cost of capital to the firm.

When the error range of this projection is wide, substitute methods have merits.

The long-run rejection rate differs from the basic minimum in purpose and level. It attempts to cope with cyclical fluctuations and with rivalry among time periods by keeping the cut-off rate constant.

Exception rates are designed to compensate for differences in the accuracy of estimates of productivity in risks and for differences in strategic value. By supplying a set of handicap differentials, certain kinds of investments are sheltered from the full rigor of rate-of-return rivalry.

The theory of capital rationing, in its most rigorous form, is based on assumptions of unattainable foresight and accuracy in measurement of productivity and appraisal of risk. Constructively viewed, these assumptions set goals for empirical estimates and spur ingenuity in overcoming imperfections. Much of the practical framework of rejection rates and restricted coverage of rate-of-return rivalry represents this kind of positive application of perfectionistic theory.

Chapter V

CLASSIFICATION OF CAPITAL EXPENDITURES

IN THE PRECEDING ANALYSIS of principles of capital rationing, several kinds of rejection rates of return were examined in terms of their operating function. It was recognized there that profitability standards might be different for different categories of investment.

Some kind of logical separation of the main categories is needed, for three reasons. First, the methods for applying the general principles of measuring capital productivity will differ according to the nature of the productivity. Second, the accuracy of rate-of-return estimates varies widely among types of investment, and there are some types for which no estimate can be made at all. Third, certain overriding strategic considerations should shelter some kinds of investments from the full rigors of rate-of-return rivalry and give them preference in capital rationing. By grouping proposals in categories, the application of these differentiating considerations can be made easier and more systematic.

This chapter considers first some of the alternative bases on which investments can be classified. It next presents some simplified classification schemes that are commonly used. Finally, a classification is outlined that is useful in discussing rate-of-return estimation. Succeeding chapters will survey each of these investment categories more thoroughly to see how their productivity is measured and how they should be treated in the capital expenditure budget.

A MULTIPLE CLASSIFICATION PLAN

No classification plan for investments is useful for all purposes. A capital outlay has too many facets to be described adequately by any one of them. Each facet is in effect a dimension of the outlay and a separate basis for distinguishing different types of investments. For purposes of capital budgeting, the important dimensions, five in number, run somewhat as follows.

Source of earnings on capital. The objective of an investment is always an increase in capital earnings, and the source of the increase is an important basis of classification. In general, capital productivity arises from cost reduction, revenue expansion, risk reduction, or improvement of employee welfare. Investments could be classified into these five categories in respect to source of their earnings.

Competitive orientation. Most investments are either aggressive or defensive, depending on whether they cause competitive reactions or are themselves reactions to competitors' moves. This dual classification cuts across the five source classes above.

Form. Distinctions as to form depend on the nature of the enterprise. For a manufacturer, a useful classification of investments might be plant facilities, product-line improvements, operating methods and know-how, and market positions. These classes naturally have any number of subdivisions, some of which themselves raise distinctive problems in capital budgeting. For instance, plant investments can be subdivided into replacements, expansions, and diversifications; product-line investments are roughly either new products or product improvements; and improvements in methods and know-how involve investments in consulting services, technical education, or interoffice rapport. Market investments are the outlays needed to capture stable market shares, such as outlays for advertising or developing distributors.

Relation to technical change. Obsolescence is a major cause of investment. When it occurs in methods, cost-reducing replacement investments may result. Obsolescence of products is associated with investments for new or improved products. From a different viewpoint, two kinds of investments related to technical change may be distinguished: established, competitively mature products and methods as opposed to innovations—new ideas that are pushed into the arena by either the company or its competitors.

Strategy aspects. By the "strategic" value of an investment is meant its indirect benefits to other parts of the company. Some investments are entirely strategic—that is, they show no promise of profitability in themselves but shore up the rate of return in other products or markets or contribute to the general strength of the company. Probably the most important strategic investments are the risk reducers, but other kinds as well are discussed in Chapter IX.

As it stands, this multiple classification, with its five dimensions and the alternatives mentioned in each dimension, allows for over 250 different types of investment, and many more could be devised. Naturally, no management works with this array of distinctions. Rather, it picks and chooses according to importance in the company. Classification plans, when they exist at all, differ considerably from one company to another, but the groupings used by three companies will illustrate how management narrows the range of its budgeting problems.

ILLUSTRATIVE CLASSIFICATIONS

An automobile manufacturer classified capital expenditure proposals in the following four categories:

1. Replacement investments.
2. Expense-saving investments, generally in the form of equipment-obsolescence investments.
3. Expansion and new-business investments, lumped together, even though they are recognized as somewhat different.
4. New-model investments, which are, for the most part, tools and dies whose economic life is as short-lived as that of the model.

A petroleum company, in contrast, uses the following classification:

1. Essential investments, that is, those required by law, by contractual obligations, or to meet competitive standards of product quality. Oil-drilling investments are put in this category because they are considered essential for the company's future.
2. Replacement investments, that is, replacement of assets that wear out with other substantially similar ones (e.g., salesmen's cars and delivery trucks). These investments are also viewed as essential, since operations would break down without replacements. They do not meet profitability tests.
3. Profitability investments, which are of two main types,

expense saving and product upgrading (i.e., converting waste or low-value petroleum products into products of higher value).

4. Desirable investments, that is, low payout investments and those for which no payout can be conveniently calculated.

Another classification plan, which is used by a building-materials manufacturer, is the following:

1. Necessary replacement investments.
2. Cost-reducing investments.
3. Product-obsolescence investments.
4. New-products investments.
5. Expansion investments.
6. Working conditions improvement investments.[1]

The classification plan used in the following chapters is based on differences in methods of measuring capital productivity and the feasibility of using rate-of-return standards in the decision to invest. It runs as follows:

1. *Replacement investments.* These include both like-for-like and obsolescence replacements, but only in the plant. Since the source of productivity is essentially cost savings, distinctive and somewhat controversial problems of profit estimates are raised.

2. *Expansion investments.* The productivity of capital here is increased revenue from doing more of the same thing. Profit

---

[1] This company investigated the way in which its capital expenditure dollar was split up among the various categories of investment. It found that during the first four postwar years new and improved products took 27 percent, expansion 24 percent, cost reduction 24 percent, replacement 18 percent, and morale improvement 7 percent. But since expansion and replacement were large, the postwar period called for an abnormal allocation. As a longer-term goal, the company thinks in terms of about 40 to 50 percent for cost-reduction and replacement investment, about 40 percent for new and improved products, and about 10 percent for welfare.

estimates involve factors different from those in replacement decisions.

3. *Product-line investments.* Expenditures on new products and improvement of old products combine features of replacement and expansion investments, but the kind of data available for profit estimates requires special treatment.

4. *Strategic investments.* Although almost every investment yields benefits that seep into other parts of the company, the types put in this category are those whose whole value seems to derive from such benefits.

As a comparison with the three company plans sketched above will indicate, there is nothing uniquely valid about this plan. It is designed for a discussion of profitability estimates rather than to fit the administrative convenience of an operating concern.

Before taking up these classifications in detail, it is important to note that most capital expenditures have mixed objectives, forms, and competitive design and thus do not fit neatly into any single category. For example, a new lithographic printing press may not only expand the capacity of a printing plant, but may also improve the quality of a printer's existing product, add new products to his line (e.g., four-color jobs), and reduce cost through lower maintenance costs and technological advances that save labor. For some investments of this type, none of the several sources of earnings may be good enough individually to justify the outlay, although as a team they add up to sizable profits. Such joint earnings make it impossible to classify the investment definitively, and the rate-of-return estimate involves considerations discussed in several of the following chapters. Although such projections for multiple-purpose investments are more complex, the total earnings are in principle determinant. Even though separation of the precise amount of capital and earnings for each source is impossible, recognition of the sources of earnings is an aid in thinking through the problem.

SUMMARY

Some major aspects of investment that make one expenditure different from another have been listed. The classification is based on economic considerations and is intended to show distinctive problems of appraising propositions. It provides an outline for the next four chapters. Many other classifications are possible, based on, for example, technical characteristics or the frequency of the budgeting decision; and these have their own uses in other problems of running a business.

Chapter VI

REPLACEMENT
INVESTMENTS

DECIDING WHEN to replace equipment is a universal (and much-debated) problem. Nevertheless, many of the methods used are based on misleading oversimplifications. Occasionally, too, they contain basic and important errors of theory which hide the real issues in capital rationing or raise false bogies. Replacement investments are often made without any reference to a rate-of-return criterion. Instead, replacements are made according to preordained schedules, or they are postponed until they become "must" expenditures, or they follow some one of the cost rules discussed later in this chapter. In contrast, the view taken here is that replacement investments can and should be forced to compete for money with alternative proposals on the basis of their prospective rate of return, and that aside from intangible earnings, such as the promotional gains from good-looking equipment, there is no particular reason for favoring replacement outlays over other investments that promise higher rates of return.[1]

[1] It can be argued that the justification for makeshift rules on replacement is that economists have defaulted on the problem. The pure theory of replacement has become an elaborate exercise in mathematics, where profit-maximizing plans are determined for a variety of abstract problems, such as the optimum life span for an infinite chain of identical replacements. (For instance, G. A. D. Preinreich, "Economic Life of Industrial Equipment," *Econometrica*, Vol.

In its pure form, a replacement investment is an expenditure for new equipment that will do the same job as discarded equipment, and the earnings of replacement are entirely in the form of cost savings. This statement is, to be sure, another oversimplification of the problem, since, as many writers have stressed, equipment is almost never replaced by an identical model,[2] but is rather swept into obsolescence by technical innovations in methods and products and by shifts in company objectives. Nevertheless, the essence of the replacement problem is easiest to understand in terms of like-for-like replacement, and in this chapter the distinction between identical replacement and obsolescence replacements will therefore be used as a structure for the discussion.

The replacement problem itself narrows down to finding the least-cost method of doing a specified task and does not include deciding whether the task is worth doing. Thus, the revenue productivity of the new equipment need not be known (and often is not known) in order to make the decision. Following the fourth principle of productivity estimation discussed in

---

VIII, No. 1, July, 1940, p. 12.) In even these oversimplified models, decisions can be made only with a fantastic amount of precise information about the future.

George Terborgh, in his thorough study, *Dynamic Equipment Policy* (McGraw-Hill, New York, 1949), has proposed a more pragmatic system for bringing economically relevant factors into replacement decisions. Because he was striving for the greatest possible realism, Terborgh demonstrates the native complexity of the problem by the assumptions and shortcuts he is forced to make. Although Terborgh's system is useful in many replacement problems, it does not take a form that shows return on investment and therefore cannot be integrated into the kind of demand schedule for capital that is proposed in this book as part of an over-all capital budget scheme. The method outlined in this chapter, by making the rate of return on the replacement investment the thing to be found, is tailored more closely to the economic situation of the individual enterprise and can be easily tied into a capital rationing procedure.

2 For instance, see Ruth Mack's discussion in *The Flow of Business Funds and Consumer Purchasing Power* (Columbia University Press, 1941), p. 242.

Chapter II, the return on the replacement is its profitability relative to the best non-investment alternative. The alternative in a replacement decision is, by the nature of the problem, to continue using the old equipment. Earnings should be estimated only for the period for which the replacement is a genuine alternative. In comparing it with a plan to postpone replacement a year, the biggest difference in its favor is cost savings over another year's use of the old equipment. In years beyond the first, the cost differences wash out on average, since the replacement machine is being compared with itself. Thus, the earnings on this year's replacement *qua* replacement are made in the first year, and the investment should be made when these earnings are above the cut-off rate, provided the task in question is worth doing.

The first part of this chapter is concerned with rationing capital to replacements of the like-for-like type. In the second part, obsolescence replacements are examined.

LIKE-FOR-LIKE REPLACEMENT

Replacement of units in a fleet of motor trucks or automobiles is a good example of a like-for-like replacement problem since in many uses trucks have not changed in ways that matter for the replacement decision. To make the discussion as specific as possible, therefore, it will be stated directly in terms of motor-truck replacement.[3]

The Problem

In physical terms, the problem is whether to replace the truck partially or completely. The inherent economy of partial

[3] This analysis is based on a paper presented at the 1948 Annual Meeting of the Society of Automotive Engineers and was published in the SAE *Quarterly Transactions*, October, 1948.

replacement is that the components wear out at different rates and that preventive adjustments can delay the component replacements. The economy of replacement depends largely on balancing these obvious material cost savings against the labor cost disadvantages of piecemeal rebuilding (as compared with the mechanization and specialization of mass production of new vehicles).

When the problem of when to replace a motor vehicle is attacked from the basic capital budget approach and the principles of profits measurement outlined in Chapter II are applied, the entire problem appears in a different perspective. The problem of vehicle replacement becomes essentially an economic problem rather than a purely technical problem. To be sure, cost savings are partly governed by the mechanical condition of the truck, but no specific degree of physical dilapidation determines when one should get rid of the vehicle.

Absolute standards of mechanical condition, for example, miles traveled, are displaced by economic standards of comparative future costs. Cost savings as a ratio of required replacement investment become the economic criterion of motor-vehicle retirement. For example, instead of routine retirement of a vehicle after five years or 500,000 miles, it is replaced when cost savings yield 25 percent on the capital put into the new truck.

In administering this economic criterion, the problem of replacement becomes a problem of cost forecasting. Replacement decisions, like all investment decisions, are inevitably forward-looking. A comparison of the future costs of the old vehicle with the future costs of the new determines the profitability of the replacement investment. Cost projections are, therefore, the basis for practical replacement decisions; and

Chart 4
Relation of Annual Operating Cost to Age of Motor Truck

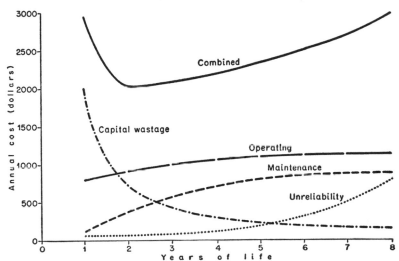

knowledge of the behavior of components of cost is the economic foundation for these projections.[4]

Graphic Analysis

The essence of the economic replacement analysis can be shown by a simple graph (Chart 4). The costs of continued use of a vehicle are a function of age and mileage. The behavior of costs with increased use is, therefore, the key to determina-

---

[4] For simplicity, the analysis summarized here is restricted. First, it is predicated on normal market conditions (i.e., availability of new trucks and market values of used vehicles normally related to new). Second, the discussion takes the viewpoint of the fleet operator and is confined to replacement of existing trucks. Third, it concentrates on concepts, principles, and the basic method and does not deal with procedures and forms. It is also confined to one-for-one replacement of a truck of equal size for substantially the same job. The methods are capable of extension, however, to meet problems involved in changing the size of trucks or transferring trucks to different jobs.

tion of the cost savings that should govern replacement. Chart 4 shows cost curves in terms of annual cost for a constant route for a hypothetical $5,000 truck.[5]

The *capital wastage cost curve* declines sharply at first and then falls off more and more gradually as the truck gets older. The curve shows the expected decline in disposal value during each year based on market price expectations.

The *operating cost curve* rises gradually at a declining rate. This cost is the sum of customary operating expenses, such as gasoline, lubricants, tires, and incidentals.

The *maintenance cost curve* represents the increase in annual maintenance and repair expenditures that will occur over most of the life of a truck.

The *unreliability cost curve* reflects an estimate of the direct and indirect losses from decline in dependability, as indicated by road breakdowns and idle time for repairs. It is presumed to rise continuously as the truck ages.

The *combined cost curve for the old truck* is the sum of the several component cost curves. It declines at first, reaches a low point, and then rises when rising operating, maintenance, and unreliability costs more than offset the declining capital wastage costs.

Average combined cost of a new truck is shown in Chart 5 by the horizontal line. It represents the expected future average annual cost of a new truck. It is computed by dividing the total estimated cost of the new truck (initial outlay and operating costs but not including interest on invested capital[6])

[5] The curves are theoretical and are designed solely to illustrate the method. They do not portray actual cost behavior of a specific truck. The shapes of actual curves differ widely among operators, depending upon operating conditions, account classification, standards of preventive maintenance, and so on.

[6] For capital budgeting purposes, the element of return on money should be viewed not as a part of capital cost but as the unknown end product of our analysis. Since it is the magnitude of the capital return that determines what

Chart 5
Cost Comparison for Truck Replacement

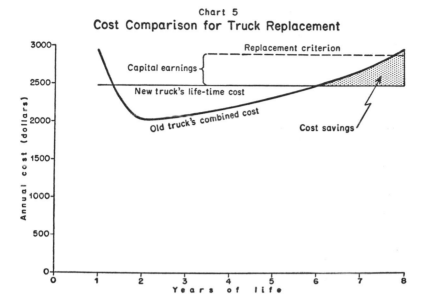

throughout its expected economic life by the number of years in its expected economic life.

The point of economic replacement is determined by prospective cost savings from replacement as a percentage of the investment required to obtain these savings. Cost savings are shown by the spread between the curve of combined cost of the old truck and the line of lifetime average cost of the new truck beyond their point of intersection. To get the rate of return on investment, this cost saving must be related to net capital outlay, that is, the original cost of the new truck minus the present disposal value of the old truck. When this rate of return equals the minimum standard return (determined

the replacement decision should be, this element is, for present purposes, not considered a cost of capital. Return on a $10,000 net investment for truck replacement is the cost savings. If they were $2,000 a year, the investment return would be 20 percent.

by the profitability of alternative uses of company capital funds), then it is economically sound to make the replacement investment.

Cost Concepts

To apply this conceptual model requires digging into the concepts and estimating methods upon which the method sketched above is built.

Future costs. For estimating capital earnings of a truck replacement, it is not past costs but future costs that are relevant. True, the records of historical cost are valuable for making this estimate, but they are valuable only to the extent that past costs and present costs can serve as a guide for estimating future costs.

In the case of recurring costs, such as maintenance, losses from breakdowns, gasoline, tires, and other operating items, the costs that were incurred in the past serve as a valid starting point for estimating costs that will be incurred in the future. Past costs of one specific truck, however, are not necessarily the best guide. The average cost of a number of trucks under similar operating conditions probably constitutes a better indication of the cost that will be incurred in the future. These averages need to be adjusted to foreseeable changes in wage rates, materials prices, and so on.[7]

Cost unit for comparison. Should the cost unit for comparison of old and new trucks be cost per year, per mile, or per service unit? Each of these cost units is satisfactory under some circumstances.

Cost per service unit (i.e., ton-mile) is usually more adapt-

[7] According to *The Minneapolis Project* (cited in Footnote 2, Chapter I), it is a rare company that tries to make a complete forecast of the cost effects of replacement. The most important omissions found in that investigation were said to be obsolescence and tax effects.

able to a variety of route conditions, but even so it fails to reflect them completely, and it often is less closely related to truck cost behavior than to some other unit. If size balance of the fleet has been substantially attained and replacement is confined to trucks of equal size for approximately the same route, then cost per year is an adequate basis for a comparison of future costs of the old and new truck. For simplicity, the analysis is developed here in terms of cost per year, but the method is equally valid when cost per year is translated into cost per mile or cost per relevant service unit, in order to calculate replacement savings when the replacement differs in capacity or expected output. However, since the estimate of capital earnings that is used for capital budgeting must take the form of rate of return if a cut-off rate is to be applied, the ultimate form must relate capital to cost savings per year, rather than per output unit, so that an estimate of output rate is necessary.

Averaging the span for new-truck costs. To make a valid comparison for purposes of a replacement decision, all costs of the new truck must be lifetime averages. Why? If the cost of operating an old truck for the next year were compared with the cost of a new truck for the first year of its life, the resulting conclusions would be thoroughly misleading. It is incorrect to consider only the costs that will be incurred early in the new truck's life, when maintenance and repair charges, for example, are known to be low. The decision to keep the old truck in operation makes only a short-period commitment to use the old truck for another year or even less; but the alternative decision to buy a new truck makes a long-term commitment to incur costs of running this new truck throughout its economic life. You are committed to the whole course of the maintenance curve, not just to its low initial phase. It is, therefore, the lifetime average level of the curve that is relevant for the new truck.[8]

The economic life of the new truck is unknown; yet it must be forecast for this and other purposes. Economic life varies not only among makes but also among users, depending upon type of service and standards of preventive maintenance. Ultimately, it depends also upon the way the replacement decision is made.

To estimate economic life, it is necessary to consider probable obsolescence. This involves a guess at the age (in years or miles) at which cost savings (of an unborn new truck) will give a high enough payout to justify replacement of the truck you now consider buying. It is obviously impossible to do this accurately, yet it will be better done if we recognize the concept we are guessing at. Actually this is done, or should be done, each time a depreciation rate is set. Probably the only sure way to find the point of economic replacement by experience is to go past it. War conditions have given some operators this instructive experience, so that they have a historical benchmark for estimating future economic life, to be modified for changed conditions.

If past replacement experience is used as a benchmark, it should be adjusted for expected changes in prices, costs, and the rate of obsolescence. And of course experience can be a misleading guide to economic life if past replacements have been made according to irrelevant or incorrect rules. To make a forecast of the economic life of a new truck on the basis of comparative cost behavior might appear to beg the question, since average lifetime costs of the new truck will depend on how long it is used. One way to cut this Gordian knot is by

[8] The basic reason for the commitment is that in the early years the losses in market value outweigh the losses in capital value associated with rising operating and maintenance costs.

successive approximations. This consists of guessing at the new truck's probable life and seeing whether its combined-cost curve and average-cost line for this life span actually signal replacement at the end of the period. If not, further guesses are made until consistent results appear. For instance, if the new truck's life is guessed as eight years, the average-cost line may be too low and signal replacement at six years. In that case, an average cost for about seven years will actually indicate replacement at seven years, which is thus the life expectancy.

Several degrees of refinement can be used in this method. Cost curves can be based on past experience, or they can be fitted to new technology, wages, and prices. Required return on capital can be modified for foreseeable changes. The average lifetime cost line, which refers to unborn trucks that will replace the one now starting service, might be shifted for future changes in both cost behavior and life expectancies. To be sure, the adjustments are rather wild guesses, but if trends are even recognized, the estimates are probably more legitimate than the alternative assumption that the present will continue indefinitely.

The character of the problem, that is, guessing how technical progress will affect comparative cost behavior of unborn models, has been accurately sized up by George Terborgh. His replacement rule is essentially the average-minimum-cost rule, with a sophisticated method of allowing explicitly for obsolescence.[9] Such a frontal attack makes sense in logic, but it is hard to say that the method produces better guesses about the effects of future obsolescence than tinkering with the average-cost curves. Moreover, his simplified versions of the rule may

[9] *Dynamic Equipment Policy*, already cited in Footnote 1 of this chapter. Service life plays no direct part in Terborgh's system. Indeed, he indirectly makes it, rather than the return on investment, the thing to be found.

be misleading to the unwary, since the formulas are based on the stiff assumption that operating costs plus obsolescence inferiority increase through time along a straight line. The conventional average-minimum-cost rule for replacement is unrealistic for a number of reasons besides its neglect of obsolescence. Changes in demand, competitive relations, and price structure can restore value to a machine that by the minimum-cost rule has become ripe for replacement. It might thus be argued that partial mathematical refinements to minimum-cost estimates add more respectability than precision to a back-of-envelope guess and that service-life estimates on the basis of large numbers of similar trucks may after all be the most efficient data to use.

It is clear that the amount of the average lifetime cost of the new truck and, therefore, the conclusion drawn from the cost-savings comparison itself will be greatly affected by the length of span over which the average is computed. Determination of the period of probable economic life of a new truck therefore deserves the best possible forecasting.

Estimating Capital Wastage Costs

Capital wastage is the disappearance of investment value as a result of use or the passage of time. It must be taken into account to get net earnings for estimating capital productivity.

Capital wastage costs of old truck. The original acquisition cost of a truck that is now in operation is sunk and irrecoverable. It can in no way affect the future money outlays or the future real profits of the company. The depreciation charges shown on the books (although they can affect the timing of the company's recognition of its profits or losses) are similarly independent of the company's real future costs and real future profits. The acquisition cost and the accrued depreciation must be dismissed entirely from consideration, therefore, in the comparison of future costs of an old truck with future costs of a new truck. These bookkeeping values may be perfectly sound for financial bookkeeping and income tax purposes, but the book value of an old truck is of no significance in making a decision on whether or not to replace one specific truck.

The only real future capital wastage costs of a present truck will arise from the future decline in the disposal value of that truck. For example, if a truck can now be sold for $8,000 and next year for only $6,000, then the additional capital loss the company will incur by keeping that truck in operation for another year is $2,000. This holds true no matter what the cost of the truck was when originally purchased, no matter when that purchase took place, and no matter how much depreciation has been charged for financial accounting purposes.

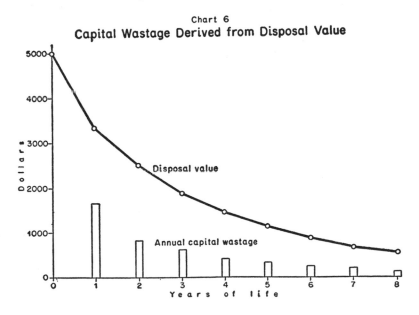

Chart 6
Capital Wastage Derived from Disposal Value

The problem of estimating capital wastage cost for the old truck consists, then, of surveying the market to see what the truck in question can now bring and estimating the amount that will be realized if the truck is kept longer (e.g., sold one year hence).

Chart 6 illustrates the kind of estimate of the behavior of normal disposal value that is needed for this purpose. It portrays disposal value of a light truck as a function of age. The curve shows estimated disposal value at the end of each designated year. The bars below are the yearly changes in the height of this curve and represent the capital wastage cost that will be incurred by retaining the old truck in operation. It is this shrinkage in market value that is relevant for determining whether the present truck should be replaced. The capital wastage curve in Chart 4 was developed in this way from market values.

Shifts in the disposal value curve itself occur frequently with changes in the general demand for trucks. These shifts complicate the analysis, but can be made part of it within the limits of accuracy in forecasting the shifts.

Chart 7 illustrates the technique. The "present function" represents the relation this year between age and disposal value, and the "future function" shows the expected relation one year hence. To estimate the future capital wastage, we must hop from the age-two value on the present function to the age-three value on the future function instead of moving down one year on a single curve, as in a normal market. Thus, on the diagram, the estimated future decline in disposal value is the sum of normal capital wastage and price level change. For very old trucks, the age decline becomes negligible and the market shifts may become relatively more significant in estimating capital wastage.

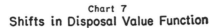

Chart 7
Shifts in Disposal Value Function

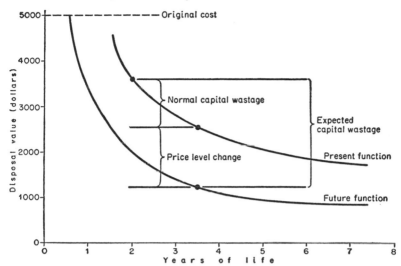

Disposal value should be determined by the most profitable alternative use that can be made of the old truck. For many kinds of equipment, the old unit can be used for less demanding work or for stand-by capacity and may have higher value here than in the secondhand or scrap market.[10]

Capital wastage of new truck. The total capital wastage cost that will be incurred by buying a new truck is its original acquisition cost less its ultimate resale value. Since the unit of cost comparison in this illustration is one year, the appropriate capital wastage cost for the new truck will be the average annual capital wastage cost over the entire period it is used in the capacity contemplated.

The two concepts of capital destruction are fully comparable

[10] Two reasons why value to the company is often higher than market value are: management knows more about machinery it has owned since birth than secondhand buyers can ever learn; and it costs more to move machinery out of the plant than it does to shift it inside.

for our purposes. Both represent the additional real costs of the alternatives being compared. The decline in the old truck's disposal value is the future cost that is attributable to the decision to keep it another year. For a new truck not yet purchased, however, the original cost (less ultimate disposal value) is the fully controllable future cost.

It is clear that a high order of judgment is involved in developing the capital wastage estimates for both old and new trucks. This does not, however, detract from the validity of this approach. It is better to have rough estimates of the right concept than accurate facts about an irrelevant concept.

Estimating Maintenance Costs

The relevant comparison of the maintenance costs of the old truck and the new truck is between expected future maintenance costs of the old truck during the next year and average annual future maintenance cost of the new truck over its expected economic life. Both items of comparison are, necessarily, estimates; but for both, the historical records of past costs will be valuable aids to projection. In most instances, the individual maintenance cost records for the old truck will be less valid as a basis for estimate than will the average past maintenance costs for a number of similar trucks in similar operating circumstances. These past costs, even though they are averages, should not, however, be taken as estimates themselves. Rather, they are starting points only, which need to be modified, adjusted, and improved in the light of whatever additional knowledge and judgment are available at the time of the estimate. Changes in wage rates, in parts prices, and in routes, all are factors that will affect future costs and should be taken into account in developing the estimate.

Maintenance for old truck. In estimating the expected

maintenance for the old truck during the next twelve months, it is well to separate major repairs from recurring maintenance. The cost of a contemplated major repair should be amortized over the expected life of that repair job to obtain its annual average cost. Sometimes the added life can best be estimated in mileage, then converted to years.[11] The estimate of recurring maintenance expected for the next year can be developed from life-cycle curves for similar trucks in the same service. These must be adjusted to reflect wage rates and parts prices expected during the next year. This actual figure needs also to be modified to take account of the history and condition of the individual truck under consideration.

Maintenance costs probably do not increase indefinitely with age. The average age of parts does not continue to increase after the truck has been properly maintained over several hundred thousand miles.

Maintenance for new truck. For the new truck an estimate of lifetime average annual maintenance cost is needed. It should be built up by adding estimates of maintenance costs during each of the years of expected service. These estimates will include anticipated major overhauls as well as all recurring maintenance and repair expense. In developing this estimate, consideration should be given to average maintenance expense of similar trucks in their various years of service in the past, but adjustments should be made to give effect to expected price levels, wage rates, labor efficiency, and shop conditions. Maintenance inaccessibility, which is characteristic of many

[11] In practice, this may become complex for trucks as well as other equipment. Certain repairs are a function of engine-miles, others a function of road-miles, and still others a function solely of age. The complicating factor is that these repairs are recurrent at different mileage and time intervals up to perhaps 250,000 engine-miles and 15 to 20 years. This precludes any plateauing of the maintenance cost curve until these maxima of mileage and age have been passed.

new models, must also modify the maintenance estimate based on past experience.[12] This lifetime total of maintenance expense should then be averaged over the expected life of the truck.

Estimating Operating Costs

The expected cost of gas and oil for the old truck during the next twelve months can best be determined by first estimating a per-mile cost and then multiplying the per-mile cost by the expected annual mileage. Past costs of the same truck and average costs of similar trucks in similar operating conditions will serve as a basis for estimate. Tire cost should also be estimated on the basis of per-mile costs. For new trucks, a lifetime average should be developed by parallel methods.

Many fleet operators find that operating costs (gas, oil, and tires) rise only slightly with truck age. Much depends on maintenance and care standards. Omission of these costs from the replacement comparison is a warranted simplification if this cost curve rises only slightly. Estimating errors of other costs that play a larger part in the replacement decision may swamp the operating cost differences. However, if future new trucks promise significant fuel savings, omission of these costs will make the test fail to detect operating cost obsolescence.

Estimating Unreliability Cost

Older trucks may be more unreliable. Losses resulting from truck breakdowns or other idle time occasioned by lay-ups for

[12] Another important factor is the system of maintenance in effect. The analysis may indicate that a saving can be effected by a reduction of the maintenance force. But if existing policies or contracts make such a reduction impossible, the saving obviously cannot be made. This is not a hypothetical case as several fleets have been in this position.

repairs should, therefore, be included in the comparison. Developing estimates of this cost will involve two steps: first, estimating the idle time in terms of days and, second, placing a money valuation on the losses, largely on idle time, in the form of a per-idle-day cost. The first step is comparatively easy if good records of past experience are available. Since dependability will be affected by maintenance standards, changes must be reflected. The second step requires much guesswork, for the indirect costs should be included, and they are often large and hard to quantify. One approach is to use the day costs of a comparable unit from the relief fleet. Another is to take the market rental figure. To these must be added costs of idle crew, towing, and so on, for on-the-road breakdowns.

Unreliability costs may make such an important difference that even a rough evaluation is preferable to omission of the cost from the comparison.

Annual Earnings

A one-year cost comparison using the foregoing estimates of cost will provide the answer to the question of whether replacement is justified on the basis of capital earnings in the form of future cost savings. In general terms, the answer can be stated thus: The present truck should be replaced if its expected costs (both capital and operating) during the next year will be enough higher than the average annual costs (both capital and operating) of a new truck to yield an adequate cost-savings return on capital. Otherwise, the present truck should be retained and kept in operation.[13]

[13] An "adequate" return on capital should be different for different companies and might also vary from time to time for the same company for reasons discussed in the preceding chapters.

Amount of Investment

Before an earnings rate can be established, the amount of capital represented by the replacement investment must first be determined. This can be obtained by finding total outlay for the new asset (including all acquisition and installation charges) and subtracting from this the present disposal value of the asset displaced by the new acquisition. This is the amount of money on which the company will forego earnings elsewhere if the truck is now replaced. This concept of net investment is not universally accepted. Some companies take half of this amount as their concept of the average amount invested over the life of the asset. And sometimes the salvage value that is deducted to get the initial investment is that of the new asset rather than that of the displaced one. That is, investment is equated with the amount of cost to be depreciated over the life of the new asset. Only when replacement is like-for-like and when the price level is stable will the concepts be equal. If a Chevrolet truck is being replaced by a Mack and if inflation is in prospect, the two notions would yield quite different estimates of the amount invested. There are a number of reasons for favoring the concept of a new truck less disposal value of the old truck:

1. Since the earnings are cost savings in the period (usually a year) before the replacement question comes up again, they should be related to the investment tied up during that period, that is, approximately the initial outlay.

2. The annual saving is a comparative figure, representing the superior efficiency of the new truck over the old. The outlay to which it is related should also be a comparative figure, therefore, showing the additional investment required to achieve this saving.

3. The current disposal value of the old truck is the amount

of capital which the company will receive if the old truck is replaced and is thus the capital invested in the old truck.

4. The eventual liquidation value of the new truck when it is replaced many years hence is relevant only for determining the depreciable total from which to calculate annual capital wastage, not for determining the investment involved.

5. The book value of the old truck is not relevant for determining the net amount of present investment. If the truck were sold and replaced with a new one, not the book value but the present disposal value would become available for investment elsewhere.

Frequency of Replacement Test

When should a replacement test be made? No rigid rule can be set up. Probably the best guide is an understanding of the underlying economics of the retirement test, coupled with intimate knowledge of the truck's condition, since this will indicate when it appears sufficiently likely that a new truck will pay out to warrant a cost comparison analysis. Except for "lemons," replacement need not normally be investigated until the truck is near the end of its forecast economic life (e.g., three fourths depreciated). It is desirable to check it again about once a year. This routine should be set aside and a replacement analysis should be made when a major overhaul is contemplated, when the cost of maintenance, wages, and parts rises drastically, when a dramatically new model becomes available, or when the market price of used trucks appears likely to fall very fast.

Other Methods of Deciding on Replacement

Up to this point the philosophy and principles of the capital productivity approach have been examined, and its application to replacement of motor vehicles has been worked out. Against this background let us now look at a representative sample of the many other methods that have been advocated and used for making this replacement determination. These sample methods, designated by their replacement criterion, are:

1. Replace every X years or Y miles.
2. Replace when the vehicle is fully depreciated.
3. Replace when the maintenance cost of the old vehicle exceeds the new vehicle's depreciation charge and maintenance.
4. Replace when the unit cost of the old vehicle is lowest.
5. Replace when the vehicle is "worn out beyond repair."

1. *Replace every X years or Y miles.* Replacement on the basis of fixed time or mileage life apparently had rather wide acceptance in the past and is still the standard for many laymen in deciding when to turn in a private automobile. This method now has little standing among economic realists. Presumably this rule descends from the long experience and shrewd analysis of some forgotten forebear, but it usually has little to do with current operating conditions, and the ancient analysis may not have been as shrewd as it should have been. Moreover, the condition of a truck and the cost of its continued operation are not solely a function of age or of mileage. They depend also on the kind of work a truck does and the kind of preventive maintenance it has had. Cost behavior differs greatly among individual vehicles under apparently similar work and repair conditions.

The fixed-life method takes no account of comparative costs or of the earnings on investment represented by cost savings. It ignores the price and the productivity of the new truck, which are vital considerations in an economic replacement decision.

2. *Replace when the vehicle is fully depreciated.* As a result

of the shortage of new motor equipment during the war, thousands of operators had the enlightening experience of running equipment long past the point when it was fully written off. Their cost experience would astound a devout adherent to the "fully depreciated" persuasion.

What is depreciation really? Depreciation is a book cost which, at best, reflects somebody's guess at the probable economic life of a new truck. It is difficult to forecast accurately, since it depends on many unknowns, including the future profitability of capital in alternative uses. At worst, depreciation is a guess at some irrelevant concept, such as physical durability, and is distorted by the income tax regulations and influenced by company notions of "conservatism."

The essential fallacy of this book-value approach to replacement is that the status of the old truck's depreciation reserve tells nothing about the real costs of continuing to operate the truck or about the prospective capital and operating costs of embarking upon the life cycle of a new truck. Straight-line depreciation makes no attempt to follow the curve of economic value through the life of the truck, but aims straight for a presumptive salvage value at an approximate date. Real capital wastage costs can be measured only by the difference between what you can get for your truck now and later. Neither the book value nor the depreciation rate of the old truck provides a valid measure of the capital wastage cost of a new truck of today's design and durability.

Finally, the book-value method makes no attempt to compare the future costs of the old and new trucks and hence takes no account of the earnings that can be expected on investment.

3. *Replace when the maintenance cost of the old vehicle exceeds the new vehicle's depreciation charge and mainte-*

nance. This ingenious solution is based on several implicit assumptions. The first is that operating costs (gas, lubricants, tires, incidentals) will be the same for the new truck as for the old. This assumption may be substantially correct, but it needs to be re-examined in each instance. The second assumption is that the market value of the old truck is zero and that there is no capital wastage on it. For some specialized and hard-to-move equipment this assumption may be true, but the replacement rule is frequently extended to marketable assets where the assumption is badly misleading. The third assumption is that the capital wastage cost of the new truck will be accurately reflected by depreciation of its original cost. This premise is likely to be invalidated by the rise of truck prices and by changed durability. Thus, the method of estimating savings is founded on assumptions that will not stand up against the rigorous economic criterion of a comparison of future costs.

Even when all these assumptions are substantially true, the maintenance-depreciation-equality method is defective because it fails to take adequate account of return on investment. It prescribes the purchase of new trucks whenever *any* cost savings are indicated. It is not enough to show some savings over continued operation of the old truck. There must be a prospect of enough savings to yield an acceptable return on the new truck investment.

4. *Replace when the unit cost of the old vehicle is lowest.* The chief defect of this minimum-cost replacement criterion was indicated by the analysis sketched in Chart 5. It is not the shape of the cost curve of the old truck, but its level that is relevant. The point at which the decline of capital wastage cost is just canceled by the rise of maintenance and other costs is a diagrammatically interesting point, but it has no economic significance for a replacement decision. As a matter of fact, there is no point on the cost curve of the old truck which,

considered alone, provides a criterion of when to replace. Only when this curve is compared with the cost of the alternative course (namely, the average lifetime cost of the new truck) does it provide any basis for making a replacement decision. Only then can the cost projection be used to measure future cost savings and thus make it possible to apply a profitability test to the contemplated investment. The low point (or any other point, for that matter) on the cost curve of the old truck, therefore, does not provide an economically sound replacement criterion.

In applying this minimum-cost replacement criterion, capital wastage costs are typically measured by book depreciation, which is likely to be quite different from the capital wastage measured in the market terms just discussed. The resulting cost curve will have a different shape, but the use of its low point as a replacement criterion will be no more valid.

5. *Replace when the vehicle is "worn out beyond repair."* "Beyond repair" is both a physical fiction and an economic fallacy. A truck can always be repaired if enough money is put into it. The managerial problem is whether this cost is too much. The answer can be found only by a comparison of the additional cost of propping up the old machine with the full lifetime costs of the new truck that will replace it. Only when the future cost saving provides an acceptable return on net investment is it economical to retire the truck. To be sure, the mechanical condition of the truck provides indispensable data for projecting the cost saving—but it cannot provide the replacement criterion.

Aversion for Capital Return Replacement

The widespread use for various kinds of equipment of plans like those discussed above for truck replacement policy indicates general aversion for making replacement investments meet a rate-of-return test in competition with alternative disposition of capital funds. In many capital expenditure plans, replacement investments are, in effect, given top priority. They are raised above rate-of-return competition and classified as "necessary."

What are the explanations and justifications for this kind of treatment? First, possibly a rate-of-return test is applied to replacement investments informally and at lower executive levels during the process of deciding whether or not the operating unit should request a particular replacement as "necessary." Second, possibly the hazard that the continued use of old equipment may cause product quality to slip is a transcending consideration. This factor cannot usually be adequately reflected in the earnings estimates of replacement equipment, yet it may have great weight. Third, possibly there is a justified belief that the losses from an inferior replacement criterion do not offset the costs of better capital rationing in this area. The amount lost by replacing equipment before or after it would be justified by a rate-of-return rivalry with alternative uses of capital may be small compared with the cost of using scarce executive time to screen replacement investments by a capital productivity test.

Limitations of Capital Earnings Method

No method of determining when to replace a vehicle is without its limitations.

Now that the defects of other methods have been cited, what about the limitations of the capital earnings method advocated in this book? The limitations summarized below are not all peculiar to this method. Most apply with equal or greater force to other methods. They are just more apparent here, since cost forecasting is explicit and conscious.

Errors of estimating costs. Since the replacement criteria are forward-looking, the analysis is based on projections. These projections of future costs will have error margins. The size of these estimating errors will depend in part on how much knowledge is available on past patterns of cost behavior and in part on the ability to forecast the impact of future changes in conditions. Nevertheless, less error will result from moderately good estimates of a correct concept than from the fictitious accuracy of precise figures on an irrelevant concept, which, it seems, is the alternative to this approach.

Errors of estimating economic life. The estimate of the lifetime unit cost of the new truck hinges on the accuracy of the projection of the length of its economic life. Dependent as it is on future durability, maintenance cost, and obsolescence, this mortality estimate is bound to be inexact, but this source of error is common to every method that takes account of depreciation.

Need for research and analysis. To make good cost projections requires some research in cost behavior, based on records of past performance. The records, however, need not be different or more detailed than are needed for other purposes. The only change is to subject them to economic and statistical analysis. The "economic" method also requires paper-work analysis of individual vehicles to reach a replacement decision, but this is a small cost when so much is at stake. Actually, the entire replacement analysis can be put on a one-page form.

Need for training. To get the full benefits of this replacement plan, all the people who use it must know what they are doing and why. They must have some understanding of the economic analysis and capital budgeting concepts on which the plan is based. This requires education, which costs money and causes headaches.

OBSOLESCENCE REPLACEMENT

In the category of obsolescence investments are replacements caused by advances in production techniques. (Investments made because of obsolescence of the company's own products—e.g., style, quality, or engineering design—are classified in the "product improvement" category, even though they are caused ultimately by obsolescence.)

Obsolescence investments are similar to like-for-like replacement in that the source of productivity of capital is savings in costs. Obsolescence investments differ from replacement investments in that the new equipment's cost superiority springs from technical developments rather than from sheer aging; if the innovation had not occurred, like-for-like replacement of the old equipment would not have shown an adequate capital return. Occasionally, sudden discoveries can justify the retirement of brand-new equipment as obsolete. Obsolescence is not absolute; it depends upon the equipment's productivity in the particular application and also upon the company's standards of effective minimum return. Hence, a piece of equipment will be obsolete for some companies but not for others and obsolete for the same company at one stage of the business cycle and not at another.

Obsolescence investments lend themselves admirably to objective capital productivity measurement and rationing. Indeed, some companies confine the ranking of earnings to this category of investment and consider all other categories as special cases exempt from capital productivity rivalry. Essentially, the application of the general principles discussed in Chapter II to the measurement of the rate of return on equipment-obsolescence investments involves the same process as that described above for motor-vehicle replacement. There are, however, differences of degree in the importance of various constituent estimates. Two striking differences occur in labor-saving estimates and economic life expectancy estimates.

Management runs the danger of being too optimistic about the labor savings that will actually be obtained from advanced equipment. The impact of an informal slowdown must be taken into account. Moreover, since labor must usually get a part of the gains either in higher pay or in lower exertion, or both, the necessity for paying the kind of wage incentives that will get the full potential productivity from the equipment should enter into the calculations. Furthermore, new equipment usually has higher hazards of breakdown and defect than equipment that is more mature technologically.

Guessing the probable economic life of the equipment whose adoption is at issue is one of the most difficult problems of measuring capital productivity. In a sense, obsolescence estimates enter at two levels. First, the test of whether or not the old model should be superseded by the new equipment is in essence a test of whether the old is now obsolete. But to apply this test, the time at which the new equipment will in turn become obsolete must be projected. Only in this way is it possible to determine the economic life of the new and thus compare its average lifetime cost with the marginal cost of keeping the old. Thus, a second level of obsolescence estimates enters, which involves expectations about the unknown new technological developments that may shorten the economic life expectancy of the new equipment. Sometimes this estimate of the life span of the new equipment is easy, as in the new-model investments of automobile companies where the lifetime is clearly no greater than that of the product model. But usually this mortality prediction is quite difficult and necessarily conjectural.

These two pure types of investment—replacement and obsolescence—produce capital earnings by lowering costs. Some executives think that obsolescence investments should have standards of minimum earnings different from those of other investment proposals. In some respects an obsolescence investment should be preferred to a new-product investment that promises an equal earnings rate, partly because the obsolescence earnings projection is likely to be more accurate (and if wrong is likely to err in the direction of conservatism) and partly because it is generally more important to keep abreast of competitors technologically than it is to expand the product-line coverage. On the other hand, some new ventures serve as an insurance on the company's future. Under these circumstances, indirect and immeasurable benefits may make the new product clearly more profitable than an obsolescence investment of equal apparent productivity. For example, an electrical company might prefer a new-product investment in the development of television to an equally profitable obsolescence investment in the manufacture of radios.

SUMMARY

A replacement investment is an outlay for new equipment that will do the same job as discarded equipment. In its pure form, it is intended solely to produce cost savings. Two kinds of replacement investments can be distinguished, like-for-like replacement, where the savings result primarily from operating inferiorities caused by physical wear and tear, and obsolescence replacements, where the savings are the result of technical progress. For both types, the source of earnings is prospective cost savings.

Replacement decisions, like all investment decisions, are inevitably forward-looking. The pivotal comparison is between the future costs of the old equipment and the future cost of the new, and the problem of estimating the return breaks down into cost forecasting focused upon ferreting out the differences in future costs between the two contemplated courses of action.

In this kind of calculation, comparison of future capital wastage costs presents unusual difficulties in both concept and measurement. Capital wastage for the existing equipment is the future decline in its disposal value. The original acquisition cost of the old machine is sunk, irrecoverable, and totally irrelevant. The depreciation charges shown on the books are similarly independent of the company's real future costs and future replacement earnings. These bookkeeping values, though useful for income measurement, have no significance for the replacement decision.

Capital wastage for the new truck over its lifetime is its prospective acquisition cost, less its ultimate resale value. Since the investment commitment has not yet been made, this total decline in value is relevant for the decision. The hard problem is to estimate the probable economic life of the new equipment. This involves a guess as to when it, in turn, will become obsolete. This guess lies at the heart of the replacement decision, even though most methods of deciding on replacement of equipment ignore it. Projection of other elements of cost for the new and the old equipment presents no serious conceptual difficulties. A capital earnings criterion of replacement is the essence of the method advocated here. The cost savings revealed by comparison of the future costs of keeping versus replacing the truck must be high enough to produce a rate of return on the amount invested to compare favorably with alternative investments and with the company's cost of capital. It is not enough that the new equipment be cheaper; it must be enough cheaper to justify tying up the capital.

Obsolescence investments are similar to like-for-like replacements in that the source of productivity of capital is savings in cost. They differ from replacement investments in that the new equipment's cost superiority springs from technical progress rather than sheer aging. Obsolescence is, of course, not absolute. It depends upon the equipment's productivity in the particular application and also upon the company's standards of effective minimum return on investment. Hence, a piece of equipment will be obsolete for some companies in some uses at some stages of the business cycle and not obsolete for other companies, other uses, and other cyclical conditions. Obsolescence investments lend themselves admirably to objective measurement of capital productivity and to rate-of-return rationing. The methods of estimating return are similar to like-for-like, but there are differences in emphasis. Two striking differences occur—labor-saving estimates and life expectancy estimates. Management runs the risk of being too optimistic about prospective labor savings from advanced technology because of inadequate allowance for informal slowdowns and for labor's bargaining power in taking a part of the gains, either in higher pay or lower exertion. Only if these concessions are made is it likely that the full potential productivity of the new equipment can be counted on.

Guessing the probable economic life of the candidate equipment has wide error margins in general when the replacement stems from technical progress rather than aging. Hence, more care must be given to projecting future life expectancies. Both types of replacement investment produce capital earnings by reducing costs, and although errors are inevitable in projecting both the future cost comparisons and the future economic life expectancies, replacement investments have a more calculable rate of return as a group than any other category of investment.

Chapter VII

EXPANSION INVESTMENTS

THE PRODUCTIVITY of capital expenditures for plant enlargement and for invasion of new markets [1] must be measured by methods different from those used to measure the productivity of cost-savings investments. Although both types involve a comparison of alternatives, the choice in cost-saving investments is between different ways of doing a job, whereas in expansion investments the question is whether or not to do the job at all. Thus, expansion investments call for a straightforward estimate of revenues and costs with and without the projected expansion. But both the cost and sales estimates present knotty forecasting problems.

On the cost side, the economies of larger plants are frequently so pronounced that it is desirable to build capacity in advance of expected sales growth. The difficult problem is to decide how far in advance. Not only are forecasts of sales growth called for, but also estimates of savings of scale. [2]

[1] Some investments that are logically in this category are not normally viewed as capital expenditures. Advertising outlays that have long-term cumulative effects are an example.

[2] Sometimes the company's own product sales can be supplemented in the early growth stages by taking on private-label business to fill capacity. For example, one of the building-materials manufacturers wanted to build a plant to make insulation board. Its sales department estimated that the most the company could sell through its own sales force by the end of two years was about half the capacity of a plant of the size needed to get scale economies comparable to those of competitors. To make the big plant feasible from the start, the company obtained a cost-plus contract for private-label manufacture for an amount that mopped up the unused capacity.

In estimating the return on expansion of production capacity, it is usually necessary to compare costs of alternative methods of attaining a given increase in output. The alternatives may take the form of buying from competitors, subcontracting, or crowding an existing plant. In principle, the profits that are relevant are the added profits over the best alternative way of getting the capacity without the investment.

Frequently, additions to capacity are made to enable the firm to reduce the number of shifts, rather than to increase its normal output. For example, automobile manufacturers after tremendous expansion investments typically run one shift in the assembly of the final product—occasionally they get up to two shifts, but never to three shifts. Perfect balance among all the subassembly and underlying operations is needed for economical three-shift assembly. Under three-shift operation there is no room to turn around: repair shutdowns, assembly bottlenecks, and so on require time leeway that is provided by one-shift or two-shift operation and denied in three-shift operation. Moreover, people dislike to work on the third (night) shift and have to be paid premium wages. Output is lower, not only because attitudes are adverse, but because workers have less ability.

Expansion investments seldom occur in pure form. Additions to capacity typically embody advanced technology which lowers costs and may improve the product as well. The new capacity sometimes demotes existing high-cost plant to stand-by status, instead of displacing it. (This is notable in public utilities.) As a consequence, safety margins for peak loads are widened.[3]

---

[3] Determination of the desirable reserve capacity, that is, optimum margins of overcapacity, is a complex economic problem. Not only does it require forecasts of trends and fluctuations of demand, but it also requires comparison of the costs of foregoing peak sales with the costs of carrying reserve capacity. A

The production costs expected for various sizes of plant can usually be estimated fairly reliably. But forecasts of sales, prices, and selling costs have extremely wide error margins, since they depend on the response of competitors and on future economic trends. Naturally, the estimate of the rate of return is no more accurate than these guesses are. Hence, in making a decision on a large expansion, the judgment of the ablest top executives is focused on the estimates of sales volume, prices, and selling costs, since these are the difficult and pivotal forecasts that govern the rate-of-return estimate. Consequently, expansion investments cannot always be put on an equal footing with cost-reducing investments in a rate-of-return rivalry.

AN ILLUSTRATION—GASOLINE STATIONS

Problems of estimating the productivity of expansion investments can be clarified by an illustration: the proposal that a major oil company acquire and operate some new service stations.[4] To measure the return on such an investment, estimates must be made of sales, gross profit margins, and marketing costs. The period of forecasting should cover the whole life of the service station and the whole term of leases and options. Since service-station investments last about 15 years, the forecasts must cut across business cycles and must take account of future changes in population, highway construction,

---

further problem is whether the reserve capacity should take the form of retained obsolete equipment or should be premature expansion in anticipation of future growth. The former has high operating costs but low carrying cost, while the latter has just the opposite. For firms whose obligation to meet peak demand is *de facto* as compulsive as that of a public utility (e.g., the steel and aluminum industries), the problem is largely statistical, as it is in utilities, since the cost aspect fades in importance.

[4] Except in Ohio, most stations owned by major companies are leased to independent operators. In order to avoid the problems of flexible rental arrangements, our illustration is confined to company-operated stations.

competitors' stations, and land values. All these factors have a bearing on service-station productivity.

Sales Volume

What pattern of sales growth can be expected for a new service station? Population growth is an important factor, but in most areas competition is the real controlling factor. Because rival stations are quick to enter the area and dilute market shares, sales in a new area tend to reach a ceiling after a few years. But this encroachment pattern is modified by the level of profit margins in the area, since competitors are interested in profits as well as in volume. Thus, volume forecasting depends to some extent on the company's own plans and expectations in pricing policy. Incremental sales from a new outlet are its gross sales minus the trade it steals from the company's other service stations in that market.[5]

Profit Margins

Determination of the added profits from the added sales volume is less simple than it appears. The estimate may be conveniently broken into two parts, added gross margins and added marketing costs. Both depend on what the company would do if the added volume were not sold through stations that it owns and operates. For some companies, the alternative is to sell the same gallonage through other channels.[6]

[5] Forecasting service-station gallonage is a highly developed art rather than a science. Some companies rely on guesses of experienced marketing executives, since these guesses bunch closely and have proved out well. Others supplement these predictions with forecasting formulas developed by empirical analysis based on such indicators as traffic flows, ease of access, visibility from the road, and community income levels. The least accurate area of service-station forecasting includes the sales and margins of auxiliary products. The ratio of such product sales to gasoline varies enormously and with no very clear relationship to locational characteristics.

[6] A major oil company may sell its gasoline unbranded as well as branded. Its

Increased sales through stations owned and operated by the company generally mean lowered sales through independently owned or operated service stations or through unbranded channels. Consequently, the added profits from added sales through owned stations can be estimated only in the light of alternative outlets for the company's products, and the return on investments in company-operated stations is measured relative to the profitability of sales through alternative channels.

The significant gross margin for an owned service station is the spread between the retail price and the wholesale price that could be charged to independent dealers, since this wholesale price is the alternative to using owned service stations. Thus, a market price rather than an intra-company transfer price is the basis for measuring return on marketing investments.[7] The relevant gross margin is the increase in margin over the best obtainable margin without the investment in retailing facilities.[8] The relevant marketing costs for a service-station investment are determined by the difference in cost of selling the gallonage through the company's own stations as opposed to selling it through alternative channels. The long-run incremental costs of direct marketing through one ad-

---

branded gasoline may be sold through three main types of retail outlets: stations owned and operated by the company; stations owned by the company, but leased to independent operators; and stations owned and operated by independent dealers. The company usually is able to sell as much unbranded gasoline as it wants to through commercial and wholesale channels at sufficient price concessions. For such a company, the service-station investment is, to a large extent, a choice between degrees of directness in marketing petroleum products.

[7] Retail margins are structurally complex and hard to forecast. The level and competitive use of margins change not only with business cycles, but also with geographical location. Gross margins are also affected by future technical developments in distribution that will change competitors' cost functions (e.g., self-service "cheapies") and thus will alter the allowable level of the company's own margins.

[8] Some kind of allowance for uncertainty may also be needed. Sales from owned stations are supposed to be more sure, but the gallonage can usually be moved through other channels at some price.

ditional station in a chain may be less than the average costs. This problem will be discussed later.

For major oil companies that buy a substantial part of their gasoline, the alternative to owning a station is to forego the gallonage. Under these circumstances, added gross margin is the whole gross margin, back to the buying point (usually a refinery). The added costs associated with the acquisition of the service station may also reach back to the buying point.

Cost Estimates

The important cost problem is to compare the incremental costs of one more outlet with the average cost of the existing owned stations. There is a strong possibility that the increase in operating costs and marketing overheads may at first be less than the over-all average of such costs. In the short run, it usually appears that no additions to overhead or operating costs will be required for a particular service station. Yet at some point in volume growth, plant and facility additions do have to be made. Usually it is impossible to predict which of the added stations will subsequently necessitate expansion of refining, transporting, and storage facilities. The danger of misusing the short-run incremental cost should be borne in mind. Viewing every addition to volume as "plus business" will lead to ruin.

The problem, then, is to estimate what these incremental costs of preceding operations and general overheads will really be in the future. Short-run incremental costs can properly be used in the uncommon situation where bulk plants and other operating facilities are operating far below efficient utilization rates and where growth of volume from existing outlets will not mop up excess capacity in the near future. For areas that will continue to have excess capacity, if the contemplated service station is not acquired, short-run incremental costs are appropriate.

SUMMARY

Expansion investments are capital expenditures designed to expand the capacity to produce and sell existing products.

The return on an expansion investment is the expected addition to profits that will result from making the investment. It is found by comparing the estimated net incremental revenue with the increment in costs and relating this added profit to the additional investment required to produce this profit.

To estimate this return requires income-statement projections of the added revenue and costs produced over the life of the investment. This projection involves appraisal of alternative ways of expanding volume without making the investment, so that comparative costs enter even into this kind of rate-of-return estimate.

The required forecasts of sales and of costs have wide uncertainty bands, as well as strategic overtones, which make precise measurement and comparison of investments of rate-of-return criteria difficult.

Chapter VIII

PRODUCT INVESTMENTS

THIS CHAPTER discusses the problems of estimating capital productivity on investments in product improvements and additions of new products to the product line. Product investments are essentially particular kinds of replacement and/or expansion investments, and rate-of-return estimates for them follow the same basic procedures. Nevertheless, in practice, product investments have sharp peculiarities that distinguish them as a separate estimating problem.

DISTINCTIVE ESTIMATING PROBLEMS

In the first place, the incremental revenues and costs are trickier to identify for product investments than for replacements and expansion. A basic purpose in adding new products is to mop up excess capacity somewhere in the organization—to make better use of one or several existing facilities. Cost changes caused by the addition are more difficult to predict than incremental costs of expansion in present operations, partly because simple expansion usually comes when capacity is filled up. Moreover, product-line changes usually make inroads into the markets of the older products of the company, either intentionally or inadvertently, but there is a question of whether old products would not have been displaced by rival companies in any case.

The second peculiarity of product investments is that they

are steeped in strategic benefits for other parts of the product line—intangible effects that are often as important as the measurable profit estimate in the decision to invest. But since direct profitability is usually the first consideration in product-investment decisions, they do not fall into the class of pure strategy investments (discussed in Chapter IX), where there is no visible profit that can be measured.

The third peculiarity is that changes in product line have greater uncertainty about their outcome; they are ventures into unexplored territory where much depends on natural ability of executives rather than on specific skills they have learned.

TYPES OF PRODUCT INVESTMENT

Product investments can be classified into two types, improvement of existing products and addition to the product line. Product-line additions are either well-known products that are new only to the company or innovations that are new to the world. In this chapter, this breakdown will be followed in discussing product investments.

There is no clean dividing line between a new product and a product improvement, but for our purposes it is enough to say an improvement is intended to displace an existing product immediately, while a new product is intended to augment the product line, at least in the short run.

Product-line policy is an area of management problems that goes much beyond the scope of this book. This chapter is concerned only with product investments that take the form of cash outlays for fairly long-term commitments and thus fit into the capital budgeting program. The most important investment in products is frequently not cash at all, but rather some bottleneck factor such as a limited supply of steel or limited management time. The basic product-line problem is to maximize return on whatever factor is most limited in supply. Cash is usually not the bottleneck for products with very short life expectancies when no long-term outlays are contemplated; nor is it the bottleneck in the longest run when the capital markets will provide funds. But for a middle range of product-line planning, cash availability may frequently be the major supply consideration. It is with this kind of product problem that the present chapter is concerned.

PRODUCT-IMPROVEMENT INVESTMENTS

Investments for improving the usability of existing products may take the form of research activity, engineering design, retooling of equipment, promotional expenses, or frequently only better quality control in production.

For capital budgeting, there is a difference between defensive improvements, that is, those required to bring the product up to competitors' products, and aggressive improvements, that is, those which improve the product beyond competitive standards. The dividing line is often hard to fix clearly, because in many industries competing products are better in some respects and worse in others. But the distinction is useful when it can be clearly drawn, because there is a compulsion to make capital expenditures which bring the product up to competitive par that is much stronger than the need to put it ahead of the parade.

Strategic considerations may be quite different on these two kinds of improvement and may depend on what position the company is aiming at in the industry quality ladder. For example, a major oil company is under strong compulsion to make whatever research and equipment investments are necessary to bring its house-brand gasoline up to the standard of major competitors, since deterioration of its brand reputation can be very costly to repair. The first department store in Chicago to put in escalators hoped that they would pay for themselves by attracting business away from competing stores. Once escalators were commonly accepted, a store with a reputation for premium service would be under strong compulsion to make this modernization investment. The source of capital productivity was the same—namely, its effect upon shifts of patronage—only the probability differs. The certainty of losing prestige and sales from below-par products and service standards is a much stronger incentive to invest than the problematic returns from aggressive improvements in products.

Investments required to keep abreast of styles are in some products even more compelling because customers can distinguish style in most products more easily than they can quality. The tremendous capital outlays of the automobile manufacturers for model changes exemplify this kind of investment. How can the rate of return of such investments be estimated? In principle, the method is clear enough. First, estimate the difference in sales with and without the contemplated product improvement; second, estimate the added net profit from this sales differential; third, relate this added profit to the capital expenditure that produces it, recognizing the limited economic life of this investment (e.g., one year for some dies); [1] fourth, estimate the added long-run profits that will result from the company's reputation for keeping abreast of styles.

In practice, forecasting sales with the precision required for this kind of rate-of-return estimate is seldom attempted. Instead, the practical course of action for most companies whose

[1] From the viewpoint of the annual income statement, an investment for a style that is certain to be usable for one year only is not properly a capital expenditure, but rather a current cost of production.

marketing strategy requires standard-quality products and services is to view investments that are required to bring products or services up to competitive par as having such high capital productivity (in view of the disastrous consequences of not making them) that they go automatically to the top of the capital productivity ladder. Investments that better competitive standards should come under review, and some kind of guess on how much short-run and long-run sales advantage will be obtained by how much capital outlay should be an integral part of the decision.[2]

NEW-PRODUCTS INVESTMENTS

In estimating the productivity of new-product investments, it is, in principle, desirable to construct what amounts to a long-term conjectural income statement. Such a statement requires, first, a forecast of probable sales and probable prices over a period of years; second, a projection of outlays for market development, including initial losses and the costs of redesigning the product to adapt it to demand; third, a projection of production costs that foresees as well as possible the size and technology of plant needed to supply a fully developed market. This income projection should, of course, cut across business cycles and envisage the long-term trend of prices and costs.

[2] A high order of judgment is required for decisions about product improvement necessary to meet competitive goals, and capital expenditure is a part, and only a small part, of the general over-all decision of what is required to keep the company competitively ahead. For example, in a new body design for an automobile, the top brains of the company participate in decisions on design from the standpoint of what is needed to attain a market share goal and keep the company's reputation for being abreast of styles. Then the top production men determine what kinds of equipment are required to produce this specified model on an economical basis. In this there is little leeway given the design of the product. Thus, the capital expenditures required for new-model equipment follow more or less automatically, particularly when the capital expenditures that will be required to carry it out are small.

In estimating costs, there is danger that some will be omitted and that some will be overstated. In general, all the costs of a going concern should be included, but they should be computed on a long-run incremental basis in the sense that they involve only the added cost of having the new product. Similarly, the investment on which the return is computed should include the added working capital, such as inventory and receivables, as well as fixed equipment. When existing land, buildings, and equipment are diverted to the new product, this investment should be included. Strictly speaking, these costs of occupation, together with other kinds of manufacturing overhead, ought to be estimated on a long-run incremental basis, but in practice such costs may be approximated by accounting allocations of full overheads. A big part of the investment outlay is the executive time, research time, advertising, and marketing work needed to develop the new product. Since these are largely fixed costs, it is in general their opportunity cost that is relevant. Although the value of foregone opportunities is hard to determine, a guess might be made by charging against the new product the cost of time devoted to it by top planners and marketers. In practice, these costs are usually treated as current expenses in the financial accounts and can only be chopped out to capitalize by meat-axe estimates.

Kinds of New Products

New-product investments may be subdivided in various ways. An important distinction, as already mentioned, must be made between established products that are new to the company and pioneering products that are new to the world. The appraisal of these two kinds of investment involves different strategy, risk, and estimating techniques. Introducing a new product necessarily entails considerable risk, and profit estimates of the kind outlined above have wide error margins. Since there are substantial differences in the estimating problems for mature-product additions and for new-product additions, they will be discussed separately below.

Mature-product additions. The problems of estimating return on investment in adding mature products to invade established markets differ from those for pioneering products. Some big companies show a cavalier and confident neglect of the costs and the profits of the market occupants in deciding whether to add the product. Primary emphasis is placed on prospects for large sales volume, long-run future, and appropriateness to the facilities and special skills of the company.

The early stages of such an investment are analogous to an investment in a research laboratory or a prestige advertising campaign. It is largely a matter of faith that earning power can eventually be developed in this area by the company—a faith reached by the combined judgment of the high command. Since the initial investment in the new venture is pretty much a gamble, no precise rate-of-return computation is made. After the venture has been going for a few years, however, and additional capital is needed for further expansion, rate-of-return criteria can be applied. Even at this stage and, more particularly, in the early stages, the pivotal estimate in the projection is not profitability, but the ultimate size of the market and the company's probable market share. A projected income statement and estimated rate of return on the new venture are never any better than this sales forecast.

The objective in invading established markets is not always aggressive. Sometimes it is primarily defensive. The most common kind of defensive move is the addition of certain basic established products that a major company thinks it needs in order to meet broad-line competition. It may be willing to make the additions even though the investment required does not show a satisfactory return directly from these products. Similarly, market rescue investments needed to hold a particular market until a more fundamental solution can be reached are sometimes justifiable even though the direct return is low. When the cost of recapturing the lost market by selling outlays would be great, a subnormal return on the market rescue investment might be justified if the foregone returns were less than the selling costs of recapture. An example of protective investment in product improvement is that made by one company to develop and produce a specially designed electric motor for window air conditioners. The company knew that the special motor would be made obsolete in two years by basic improvements then being worked out, but in the short run it faced substantial loss of business to a competitor who was using a motor of this kind. It made the investment to prevent having to spend even more money later to get back into the market.

In general, for such investments the threatened segment of the market should be regarded as marginal business, and the earnings on it should be regarded as the additional return that would be obtained by making the improvement as opposed to dropping the product. The investment should be made only if it passes the company's rejection-rate tests. If grand strategy calls for an eventual share of the market, the costs of recapture should be the minimum standard for an acceptable return on the short-run investment. That is, with this strategy, some out-of-pocket loss may be acceptable.

New-product additions. The uncertainties and hazards of introducing a true innovation to the product line are far greater than those of mature-product additions, and rate-of-return estimates are made with different considerations in mind.

The mortality rates for such products are terrifying. The experiences of organizations with venture capital to invest, such as J. H. Whitney & Company, are instructive here. This company reported that of 2,100 propositions studied, only 17 were sufficiently meritorious for the company to put money into them, and, out of this 17, only two were conspicuously successful. Five were moderately so, six were borderline failures, one was a clear failure, and three were still too young to appraise.[3] Even new products introduced by large and successful companies have high mortality. Only about one out of five such products is successful, according to a recent study.[4]

Several specific sources of uncertainty need attention in capital budgeting. First, the product itself may not be as good technically or from the consumer's standpoint as it appears. Protracted field testing is a necessary prelude to commercialization. The instances of premature introduction are numerous. The Chrysler Air-Flow design was a glaring example. Second, initial low-volume production methods are subject to rapid and unpredictable technical changes. Cost projections—the most reliable element of most profit forecasts—have wider error margins, therefore, for new products than for established products. Third, the impact of cyclical swings and fashion cycles is harder to guess, as is underlying demand. Fourth, the costs of developing the market for a striking innovation are great and hard to predict. The innovator usually has to carry the main burden of consumer education, at least in the early stages.[5] Fifth, the rate of competitive entry and imitation is

[3] "Volume and Stability of Private Investment," Subcommittee on Investment of the Joint Committee on the Economic Report (81st Congress, 2d Session, March, 1950), p. 26.

[4] "The Introduction of New Products," a survey made in 1949 by Ross Federal Research Corporation, for Peter Hilton, Inc.

[5] An example of error in estimating the time and the amount of specialized edu-

hard to predict. Distinctive specialties tend to degenerate into ordinary commodities, with a corresponding deterioration of profit margins, as competitive encroachment wipes out the salient of monopoly innovation.

These various technological, economic, and competitive uncertainties are often accentuated by the long gestation period between the basic research and the final profits of full commercialization, and these uncertainties make capital productivity estimates so tenuous that strategic considerations are often determining.

An important strategic consideration in product-line additions is to develop goodwill for other products. For example, a large electrical company recognizes that its investment in the production of betatrons and industrial X-ray equipment and its basic research in atmospheric electricity are largely justified by the contribution that these activities make to the company's general reputation. Like investments in research laboratories, these new-product investments have invisible payouts that are primarily promotional for the new-product investments.

Another kind of strategic consideration in new-product investments is the desirability of getting in on the ground floor in a pioneering area that appears likely to become important in the future. The experiments of Boeing Aircraft with trucks driven by gas turbines fall into this class.[6]

---

cation and cooperative experiment required to induce buyers to substitute new products for existing ones is found in a large company's investment of $12 million in a plant to manufacture a newly developed silicone. The plant lost money over a much longer period than had been estimated. Part of the delayed development was due to the company's failure to realize that highly specialized chemical engineers were needed to introduce the product. It originally tried to market through its regular sales organization.

[6] A more complete analysis of product-line strategy is found in Joel Dean, *Managerial Economics* (Prentice-Hall, Inc., New York, 1951), Chapter III.

SUMMARY

Product investments include both improvements in existing products and additions to the product line. Defensive product improvements have a higher order of productivity (stemming from the strategic importance of holding market share) than aggressive improvements, and capital budgeting considerations are quite different for the two types of improvement.

Investments to add products to a company's line are of two main kinds—investments for established products that are new to the company and investments for pioneering products that are new to the economy.

To measure the return on such investments involves projection of complete income statements over a period of years. These statements require forecasts of sales, prices, market development costs, and production costs.

Prospective profitability can be measured for investments to manufacture an established product somewhat more reliably than for new products. For most large companies, however, the pivotal estimate is the long-run future size of the market, and the companies are willing to take their chances on designing an acceptable product, getting its costs down to competitive levels, and grabbing an adequate market share. Thus, precise estimates of prospective return are probably not controlling considerations, at least in the initial stages.

For pioneering products, profit projections have such wide error ranges by reason of the technical, marketing, and competitive uncertainties that forecasts of rate of return give a false impression of precision. Consequently, in making such investments, a high order of judgment of the critical forecasting factors is required. And the *reliability* of these estimates is often the pivotal consideration, rather than the *level* of return calculated from these uncertain estimates.

For both mature and pioneering products, most of the factors in the product-line decision come to a focus in prospective "profits" in some comprehensive sense of the word. But the factors are so difficult to measure that a consideration of their size and the weight to be given them throws many new-product investments out of the arena of rate-of-return competition.

Strategic considerations then become dominant. New-product investments may serve several kinds of strategic ends besides making money on the new product itself: they may be primarily defensive, as in the addition of products to meet full-line competition; they may be predominantly aggressive in staking out a claim in new areas such as television or nucleonics that promise a big future, or they may be primarily promotional in that a large part of their prospective return is invisible and takes the form of increased goodwill for added sales of other products. The strategy of mature-product additions is usually either defensive or a deployment of forces for aggressive action.

Chapter IX

STRATEGIC INVESTMENTS

IN THE INVESTMENT TYPES that were examined in Chapters VII and VIII, the source of productivity was either cost reduction or increased revenues. In this chapter attention is turned to the other two groups in the source classification—namely, risk-reducing investments and welfare-improving investments. These two are grouped together because they have two common characteristics. First, the return on investment, though real enough, is hard to measure, because it is often delayed, indirect, and intangible. Hence, decisions are in large part a matter of experienced judgment or even blind faith. Second, all investments in these two categories are broadly strategic in objective; that is, their benefits are spread over many phases of company activities and stretch into the distant future. The combination of a return that is intangible and a purpose that is strategic makes it impractical to have such investments fight for funds in the arena of capital productivity against more objective investment types without some handicap allowances in profit requirements. They thus raise a budgeting problem in differential rate-of-return standards.

In determining how such investments should be appraised and how they can be compared with those whose profitability can be more accurately measured, this chapter first examines the subcategories in the risk-reducing and welfare-improving types of investment, and then discusses generally the approach to a measurement of the rate of return in so far as it can be measured, and finally suggests an approach to appraisal.

RISK-REDUCING INVESTMENTS

In our original classification scheme (Chapter V), investments were subdivided into two categories, according to competitive orientation—defensive investments and aggressive investments. Since most strategic investments have mixed objectives, it is frequently difficult to distinguish between them in particular instances on this basis. When they are fairly clean-cut, however, there is some usefulness in grouping risk-reducing investments in this manner, because the defensive ones call for a different appraisal from those that are designed primarily to stake out a new gold mine.

A good way to point up this distinction is to examine a type of risk-reducing investment that is dominantly defensive—namely, those associated with vertical integration—and then look at a kind of investment that is characteristically aggressive, namely, research investments.

Defensive Investments—Vertical Integration

A prominent characteristic of investments for vertical integration is reduction of the company's long-run hazards in a defensive manner. Investments in backward integration often have the purpose of gaining control over raw materials or production of components that the company formerly bought.

Not all integration investments are, however, strategic. The classic motive of backward integration is to produce products at a lower cost than their purchase price. When this is the purpose, the investment should go into the cost-reducing category, where the rate of return is determined by comparing purchase costs with production costs, both on an incremental basis. The investment to which this incremental profit should be related is the added investment in facilities and other aspects of the going concern required to produce this backward integration.[1]

In contrast, a strategic investment in backward integration has the purpose not of saving money on present purchasing costs, but of reducing the risks that are associated with outside supply. These risks may be quality risks or quantity risks. Much modern backward integration has been designed for the purpose of controlling the quality of the raw materials and components and thus protecting the reputation of the company. Another common risk-reducing purpose is protection against shortages of supply. During the early postwar years this motivation dominated, because supply shortages were absolute; many producers were never sure when and whether they would get another shipment. This danger of complete cut-off in raw material supply does not fit into economic doctrine, because theoretically it is always possible to get supplies by bidding up prices a little more. But theory overlooks the phenomenon of private rationing, where suppliers keep prices rigid for wide ranges of demand and dole out their product according to past purchases or some other non-price scheme. Private rationing after World War II was most famous in the steel industry, which was consequently plagued with "gray" markets, but it was also common in more competitive markets, such as lumber

[1] The notion that this kind of penuriously motivated integration should be required to earn a premium return has some merit. Reaching backward into unfamiliar industrial processes puts the company in competition with specialists in the industry who are likely to be better equipped for minimum-cost production. It also produces managerial dilution and headaches, which are hidden costs in such a move. Some firms have had such disappointing experiences with integration designed to capture suppliers' profits and save costs that they penalize such investments formally or informally in capital budgeting. Their political, as well as technological, vulnerability adds force to this argument.

and automobiles. For a paper mill, the source of earnings from an investment in pulp mills and forests might be calculated in terms of the foregone gains in market share from lack of supply of pulpwood or even loss of share to companies that do have private supplies of wood.

The more normal justification for backward integration is the long-run protection of the price position in supply markets. Although under normal conditions supplies can be acquired from expensive temporary sources when the alternative is to stop production—for example, "conversion deals" in steel— this is a weak competitive tactic, particularly when the supplier applying the price squeeze happens to be an integrated competitor. Thus, a building-materials company acquired an asbestos mine, not because it had an attractive payout, but because the acquisition protected the company against possible price squeezes from the closely held and semi-cartelized asbestos mining industry.

The rationale for strategic investment in sources of supply often depends on some kind of long-range estimate of what may happen to prices. An oil company that elects to divert a high proportion of capital investment into drillings should base that decision on conjectures about the price differentials between crude and refined products in the future. Another building-materials company made an investment in its own source of asphalt because the company anticipated long-run price increases as the petroleum industry gradually found more uses for asphalt in its burgeoning chemical operations.

Aggressive Investments—Research

Another category of risk-reducing investments is research. Such investments may be more "aggressive" than typical integration investments, but they are also defensive, since rivals also have research laboratories. Yet, the purpose is usually to keep the company out in front technologically and to profit from pushing back the frontiers of knowledge. Advertising outlays of an investment character also might go in this category, although they are not in financial accounts treated as capital expenditures.[2]

Determination of the rate of return on research investments is difficult. How can the payout for a new technical research center be projected? Conceivably, this can be done by some kind of comparison based on where the company would be 20 years from now without the research facilities or, alternatively, by computing how much it would cost to buy the same quality of research on a consulting basis. Neither of these approaches is at all feasible. Thus, aggressive strategic investments must usually be made on faith—faith, to be sure, founded on experience that research has paid out in the past and founded on the technicians' counsel that they can work better with good facilities than without them. For some research equipment, a guess can be made as to savings in scientists' working time, but more commonly it is not a matter of time savings, but of carrying out projects that would not otherwise be possible.[3]

[2] In mature industries, however, much advertising is essentially defensive, and long-run cumulative advertising may be so as much as short-run.

[3] Although results of future research are almost beyond speculation, the profitability of past research has now become an object of formal accounting estimates in some companies. Profits resulting from ideas of the research division are credited to its account, either directly if the profits are visible or by guess if they are intangible. A paper company computes net profits separately for research products and non-research products and credits the differential return to the research account. Another company credits research with one year's savings on new processes, 3 percent of sales for four years on new products, and 3 percent of sales for one year on improved products. A third company credits research in full for measurable cost savings and increased profits and credits it with from two to four times the cost of proposals that have intangible value. The credits are continued through the life of the profits, which generally are extinguished in a fairly short period by competitive encroachment. (For estimating methods, see *Management Review*, October, 1950, p. 588.)

WELFARE INVESTMENTS

The productivity of welfare investments lies in long-run reduction in labor cost through improving morale and thus reducing turnover, recruiting costs, and strike losses. These investments may be put into two subcategories, employee welfare and plant community welfare. Since most employees live in the plant city, there is some overlapping, but the benefits of community investments range much farther than just the circle of employees and merchants whose income derives from the company. Community investments offer a rich mixture of general public relations.

Examples of the employee welfare investments are cafeterias, club facilities, and safety devices. Hospitals and community centers are examples of community relations investments. For neither of these types is it possible to estimate rate of return in any but the vaguest terms, and for practical purposes it is useless to try. Of course, some such investments have high capital productivity, but there is no way of telling which have and which have not or whether the productivity of a morale-improving investment compares with that of an equipment-obsolescence investment.

This is an area in which capital budgeting must be done solely on the basis of judgment in response to pressures and opportunities. It is doubtful whether even the experience of companies that have gone overboard in this kind of investment as contrasted with those that have been niggardly is more conclusive.

APPRAISAL OF STRATEGIC INVESTMENTS

From the foregoing discussion, it is clear that rate-of-return criteria are not usually feasible for rationing funds to strategic investments. What criteria, then, can be applied? None are satisfactory. Some companies set aside some specific proportion of the total revenue stream, or the total capital budget, over a period of years. For example, one company set aside 10 percent of its postwar five-year capital budget for research-facilities investments. Over the last 20 years, it has saved out 1 percent of sales for current expenditures in product research. For morale-improving investments it set aside roughly 5 percent of its five-year capital budget. For defensive risk-reducing investments, standards were set up in terms of producing "x" percent of its major raw materials, and the minimum rate-of-return standard on such investments set substantially below the normal standard. For example, when the standard was 20 percent for equipment-obsolescence investments, timber reserves were acquired that promised only a 4 percent return.

Thus, rationing capital for these dominantly strategic investments whose productivity is imponderable falls back on judgment concerning their long-term benefits. This judgment can be codified in the form of the patterns of some definite proportion of total capital expenditures to be held out for this kind of investment over a long period of years, but there are no objective guides to what this "x" percent should be.

But even for these categories of investment, rate of return has a role in rationing. First, for investments such as defensive risk-reducing investments, where it is often possible to estimate the direct portion of capital productivity, alternative strategic investments can be made to compete with each other by specially designed rate-of-return standards. For example, 10 percent can be added for the unmeasured indirect contributions. For the others, knowledge of the alternative cost of capital for these strategic investments (the measurable productivity in the most profitable displaced equipment-obsolescence investments) may refine executive judgment by showing the cost of strategy. Then the gains of strategy can be stacked up against these foregone profits from alternative investment.

SUMMARY

Two broad groups of strategic investments may be distinguished—risk-reducing and welfare. Risk-reducing investments may be divided into two classes, defensive (e.g., producing previously purchased raw materials to protect quality, quantity, or future prices) and aggressive (positive improvement goals, e.g., technical research facilities). Welfare investments may be directed only at employees or at the entire community.

All kinds of strategic investments have two characteristics in common. Their central objective is strategic in the sense that the benefits spread over the enterprise as a whole and stretch into the distant future and are related to long-run company goals. Their rate of return is usually difficult or impossible to measure, largely because indirect benefits are imponderable.

Because of these characteristics, such investments must be sheltered from the full rigors of rate-of-return competition. This can be done by setting aside a certain proportion of planned capital expenditures for each kind of investment.

An alternative is to make modified use of rate-of-return criteria, supplemented by generous doses of "judgment." For some of these investments, a rate of return that reflects a part of their benefits can be estimated. These estimates can be thrown into the system of capital productivity rationing by applying handicapping percentages that reflect the judgment of the high command on the benefits omitted in the earnings calculation. For example, defensive investments to assure quality or quantity of materials can be given a plus 10 percent rate of return. However, this treatment can apply only to a few investments, and even in them there is no clear indication of the right "x" percent handicap.

Chapter X

CYCLICAL INVESTMENT POLICIES

IN THE FOREGOING DISCUSSION of capital rationing theory, two alternative cyclical policies were outlined for capital expenditure budgeting. The first used a fluctuating standard of minimum acceptable profitability which for the autonomous firm not only would rise and fall with variations in its cost of capital, but also would, at cyclical crests, rise significantly above its cost of capital because of the inadequacy of self-generated funds to meet boom capital demand. Hence, wide swings in the standard of marginal productivity would be contemplated. For a firm willing to supplement internal funds from outside, the swings in the cut-off rate over the cycle would be determined by fluctuations in its cost of capital, which would pulsate with conditions of the security market. Over a period similar to the last 25 years, for example, the combined cost of capital (equity and debt) for an established and large manufacturer might reasonably be expected to fluctuate between 6 percent and 40 percent. The range would differ considerably among companies.

The alternative cyclical policy is a constant rejection rate which does not fluctuate cyclically, being formulated to clear the firm's internal capital market for the cycle as a whole by balancing capital demand with self-generated supply. For the firm that raises capital funds outside, the cyclically stable rejection rate would be determined by its projection of future long-run cost of capital. For example, 15 percent might be forecasted for a manufacturer based on a study of that company's investment market experience of the last quarter century.

Either of these policies will result in wide fluctuations in the level of investment activity, since it is visible demand, which is highly volatile, rather than a vague guess about long-run demand, that determines this year's outlay. When these fluctuations are added up for all industry, they are clearly a serious destabilizing influence on the level of economic activity.

The desirability, from the standpoint of maintaining high and stable employment and national income, of reducing the amplitude of these swings in capital expenditures by private firms is clear. Business leaders have quite generally recognized that they would make an important contribution to economic stability by smoothing out cyclical fluctuation in their capital expenditures, but the practical question for each firm to face is how far it can go in this direction without incurring too much cost and risk.

This chapter discusses the firm's capital budgeting problems in coping with capital supply and demand curves. The principal question is the extent to which a more stable pattern of investment can be profitable for the individual enterprise, that is, its gains and limitations in making more of its capital outlays in depressions and less in prosperity. As a framework for the discussion, we assume continued fluctuations in general business activity and no major changes in the government's powers and policies concerning business cycles. In sketching the way in which a firm might approach this problem, the possible gains from stability will first be outlined. Second, the losses from changing the cyclical pattern will be studied. And third, some of the administrative problems will be examined.

Instead of the cosmic view usually taken of causes of fluctuations in capital formation, we shall take a firm's eye view of the sources of instability. This is consistent with the worm's eye view of economics taken throughout this book, and it results in a prospect quite different from the panoramic vistas of general economic analysis.

GAINS FROM STABILIZING CAPITAL EXPENDITURES

In deciding how far to go along the road of smoothing out cycles in its capital expenditures, a company must balance gains against costs and losses. The firm might have indirect gains as well as direct.

Indirect gains arise to the degree that stabilization of the individual firm's capital expenditures brings about more stability of the economy as a whole; thus, such stabilization reduces fluctuations in demand for the firm's products and permits more predictable and stable operations. If all firms were able and willing to make their capital expenditure budget more stable or even contra-cyclical, there is no doubt that a substantial reduction of general economic fluctuations would result. But this bread-upon-the-waters view of the matter depends upon widespread acceptance, which, without compulsive incentives, such as subsidies, is highly unlikely. Hence, the indirect benefits as a practical matter are negligible.[1]

The direct gains take four forms: price level savings in

---

[1] The possibility of stabilizing capital expenditures differs among firms. In general, those with rapid and foreseeable growth and financial strength are most able to make such changes. But even for them, a voluntary reduction of earnings and increase of risks would be involved.

acquisition costs and construction costs by increasing the proportion of investments made at cyclically low price levels; cost savings that come with unhurried planning, buying, and development of new facilities; capacity availability in the early stages of recovery; and smaller errors of optimism in appraising capital productivity than frequently characterize boom-time estimates of rate of return.

Some indication of the savings from cyclical price cuts can be found in the *Engineering News Record* index of construction costs and the Marshall-Stevens index of equipment costs. The ENR index, for example, fell by 30 percent from 1920 to 1922 and by 24 percent from 1929 to 1932. However, in mild depressions such as those of 1923–24, 1926–27, and 1937–38, construction costs fell very little (less than 2 percent). In the Marshall-Stevens index, equipment costs showed smaller declines than construction costs in general, although informal concessions below quoted prices usually mean that such an index understates the amplitude of fluctuations.

When activity is low, the engineering staff can devote more than enough time to long-run plans, suppliers give a maximum of free service extras on purchases, construction force may have higher productivity, and management can watch over the project closely. The result is better quality, better scheduling, and better integration of the new investment into the existing organization.

Advantages from starting expansion programs in time to provide capacity when needed in a period of prosperity derive from the long gestation periods typical of big construction jobs. To realize these advantages fully, it is necessary to forecast the rate of recovery from the depression. Moreover, they are often whittled down when the bottleneck factor is not plant capacity but some other input factor, such as steel or skilled labor. Nevertheless, a part of the gain comes from having a more modern and lower-cost plant rather than solely from bigger capacity. In many industries, the aggregate plant capacity is sufficient for crests of booms, but is arrayed in a steep cost-ladder of obsolescence.

COSTS OF STABILIZED INVESTMENT

Offsetting these gains of stabilization outlined above is a formidable list of extra costs in a stabilized investment program. The decision on cyclical policy depends on the relative importance of gains and losses, unless the company is to take on its own shoulders the profitless burden of stabilizing the economy.

There are two parts to this problem—the decision in boom periods to postpone outlays until the following recession and the slump-period decision to invest now rather than in the upswing.

Viewed at the crest of the cycle, many expenditures cannot be postponed during peak activity without dire strategic consequences. Defensive investments to fend off competitors who are invading markets with new products fall into this category. Product obsolescence is a particularly important deterrent to cyclical stability where style changes are frequent and involve heavy outlays. The automobile industry presents a sterling example. For some manufacturers, about half of the capital expenditures in a normal year are for tools that are intimately tied into the model produced that year, and the amounts of tools are closely related to boom production volume. If the company tried to tool up for a model for years ahead of time, it could not possibly foresee style changes or technical improvements well enough to be confident that the equipment would not be obsolete before it was used.

There are also compelling strategic reasons for making the investment necessary in prosperity to fill the current volume of orders, since long delivery delays shift customers to competitors who may be able to hang on to them far into a recession. Many companies in the postwar boom decided to build additional plant capacity at penalty prices in order to expand or hold market share when it was virtually determined by productive capacity and when the share thus captured had a good chance of being retained. For example, there was a stage when capacity to produce governed automobile market share, and the proved propensity of motorists to trade in on the same brand assured retention of market share if future models could be kept competitive. In these instances, plant additions were an economical way to buy market share as opposed to the slow, grueling method of battling for it in a buyers' market. The costs of getting that market position in the normal competitive tussle would have to be overshadowed by lower acquisition costs in depression and by the possibility that postponement would make possible advanced technology.

From the viewpoint of the trough of the cycle, what are the costs of spending now rather than when things start looking up? They can be roughly grouped as follows:

1. Reduction in present worth of a cyclically fluctuating stream of earnings.
2. Increased risks of obsolescence of both products and processes.
3. Higher costs of funds.
4. Increased risks of inadequate liquidity.
5. Hazards of imperfect foresight.[2]

[2] What traits of a particular investment influence the extent of loss from post-ponement or anticipation? The following are suggested: (1) The degree of

1. *Reduction in present worth.* The gross profits from an investment will usually be higher in prosperity years than in depression. Since the value of an income dollar at a distant date is less than at a near date, the value of an investment is less when its near years are lean than when they are fat. This can be measured by discounting this uneven stream of expected income down to its present value at some rate of interest. When an investment is made in prosperity, the near years are big-profit years and also are weighted heavily in the discounted value. Consequently, if the acquisition costs of the investment are the same in prosperity as in depression, the present value of its stream of profits will be higher if it is acquired in prosperity than if it is acquired in depression.

The amount of this disparity in present value will depend upon three things: the amplitude of the fluctuations in profits from depression to prosperity; the rate at which it is discounted; and the length of the projected economic life of the asset. Table III illustrates the impact of the first two of these forces on cyclical shifts in the present value of an investment. The effect of the third is a complicated relation between the life of the investment and the length of the cycle, and a description of it is beyond the scope of this discussion.

Table III measures only the superiority of prosperity invest-

---

uncertainty in forecasting technical advances. When it is hard to guess the rate of obsolescence in the candidate equipment, there may be considerable range of choice as to when to make the investment, since the economic life of the new equipment determines whether or not the present equipment is obsolete. (2) The richness of the return. One of the costs of postponements is foregone earnings. An investment that shows 50 percent earnings can rarely be put off. (3) How catastrophic the alternative is. Investments that are sometimes put in the "necessary replacement" category involve dire consequences if deferred. In a sense, this merely means they have tremendous productivity and thus fall into the preceding category. (4) How perishable the opportunity is. Some kinds of strategic investments lose all prospective profitability if they are not made at cyclical peaks or at the time when the competitive necessity for them arises.

Table III

CYCLICAL SENSITIVITY IN VALUE OF A NEW INVESTMENT

	PERCENT CHANGE IN PRESENT VALUE OF INVESTMENT FROM PROSPERITY TO DEPRESSION [a]		
RATE OF DISCOUNT [b]	Amplitude of Cycles [c]		
	0.5	5.0	10.0
4%	.065	.65	1.29
10%	.40	3.96	7.76
20%	14.77	88.73	122.93

[a] Present value of investment made in prosperity minus present value of investment made in depression as percent of prosperity investment value.
[b] Rate at which future earnings are discounted to present value.
[c] Ratio of peak earnings minus trough earnings to average earnings, for example,
$$\frac{\$700 - (-\$300)}{\$200} = \frac{\$1000}{\$200} = 5.0$$

ments that results from discounting future funds. The table is based on the difference between the present value of the prospective earnings stream of an investment made at the peak of prosperity and the present value of an identical stream for the same investment made at the trough of depression (prices, technology, etc., constant). The calculation is for an investment with a 20-year life, when earnings cycles last four years. The difference in present value is expressed as a percent of present value of the investment when made at peak prosperity. Three discount rates and three amplitudes of cyclical fluctuation are used, to illustrate the range of possible effects. The relevant discount rate for a particular company is its cost of capital or opportunity cost of investment in depression. For simplicity, the calculation in Table III assumes that cost of capital is the same in prosperity and depression. It thus understates the true disparity in values, because capital costs are more likely to be lower for the prosperity investment.

To isolate the pure effect of timing on present value, a rigid assumption is made that the prospective earnings stream is a sine-wave oscillation of exactly 20 years' duration, with a four-year period. Average earnings for a cycle are assumed constant for the five cyclical periods (although the present value of average earnings is, of course, lower for later cycles than for earlier ones).

From the table it is clear that the sensitivity of the value of an investment to its cyclical timing steps up with volatility of earnings. Sensitivity to cyclical timing increases sharply with the rate of discount. For an amplitude of 5.0, the drop in value is negligible at a discount rate of 4 percent, but the present value drops 88 percent when the discount rate is 20 percent, a level that is more generally comparable to alternative earnings opportunities for capital.

The 20-year life is substantially longer than the economic life that is characteristic of modern equipment. Shorter life spans involve greater risks in cyclical timing, because small deviations from the optimum date of purchase take more value from an investment that will last through two cycles than from one that will last through five cycles.

2. *Increased risks of obsolescence.* Not only will the lean, early years give a lower value to a depression investment; they will also increase the risks of unforeseen obsolescence. A low load factor means that a replacement investment will take longer to pay out in cost savings than if it were being worked to capacity. If technology is advancing rapidly, equipment acquired years ahead in anticipation of a boom may become obsolete before it does the expected work.[3] Physical deteriora-

[3] These costs are not less real when hidden by hand-me-down idleness. Newest equipment goes into highest-grade service and hence may get used even in slack times; existing equipment sometimes gets demoted down successive ranks of stand-by status (particularly in public utilities). Premature retirement to stand-by and excessive reserve capacity are costly, too.

tion of unused capacity with the passage of time may also be a cost of stabilized capital investment. But it would rarely be a net addition to obsolescence, since most modern equipment gets out-moded before it is worn out.

3. *Higher costs of funds.* Another kind of deterrent takes the form of the higher supply cost of funds. Our analysis of the sources of funds for capital expenditure in Chapter III showed that there were pronounced cyclical swings in both internal and external availability of funds, since internal funds depend on retained earnings and dividend policy, while external funds are subject to the changes in cost and amount of capital that is offered by the market.

Aversion to debt and to outside equity financing makes many companies autonomous in capital formation, thus tying them to cyclical fluctuations in internal sources. Interestingly enough, the fluctuations in private capital formation in the past can quite largely be accounted for empirically by changes in current corporation profits and in corporation profits one year earlier.

Companies that supplement internal sources by external sources also experience shifts in their supply schedule. These come from fluctuations in the current cost of capital, particularly the violent changes in the price-earnings ratios and price-dividend yields of common stocks. Thus, most companies must expect pronounced cyclical shifts in supply of funds for capital formation, whether viewed in a market schedule sense or in terms of the enterprise's own cash-generating ability.[4] For stabilized investments, either money must be raised and

---

[4] These fluctuations can be reduced and the average cost of capital lowered by varying the proportion of debt to equity opportunistically to fit security market fashions in favored types of security. When prices of common stocks are low, bonds are a more appealing type of financing, but this kind of arbitrage is an important possibility for only a few industries such as public utilities.

saved in booms and carried over to depression, or it must be borrowed short-term in depression in anticipation of raising it in booms. Short-term borrowing for contra-cyclical investments would be for most firms impossible or extremely expensive, since it would run counter to the philosophy of commercial banking. If instead of borrowing, prosperity earnings are saved for depression spending, there is a cost of carrying funds that must be borne by interim investments and/or the depression project itself.

4. *Increased risks of inadequate liquidity.* Another kind of deterrent, which cuts across many of the preceding, is cyclical changes in liquidity preferences that stem partly from general uncertainty in periods of depression. Going against the cycle in capital expenditures requires intelligence, confidence, and courage. When things look bad, prospective earnings on capital expenditures are viewed with gloom, and the fear that cash will be needed for operations if the depression gets worse breeds timidity and compels hoarding.

5. *Hazards of imperfect foresight.* Risk from imperfect foresight as to future demand is an important deterrent. Few boards of directors would or should have the courage to authorize big capital expenditures in the depths of a depression on the expectation that expanded capacity would be needed in a later boom. Serious mistakes could be made in respect to the level and geographical pattern of sales, the character of the product, and the nature of the technology. For example, who could have foreseen in 1938 the importance of automatic transmission in automobiles today? Who can now foresee how fast television will displace radio and movies? The foregone savings in construction costs can be minor as compared with the risk from inadequate forecasts of demand and technology.

The cost of carrying unneeded plant capacity until it is needed is a deterrent to depression-period expansions that combines the obstacles discussed above. In part, it is the cost of tying up funds and foregoing other opportunities. The earnings on distant revenues must compete at their discounted present value with these other opportunities. But more important are the risks that long-range sales forecasts will prove too bold and that changes in products and technology will make the new plant obsolete before it is really put to work.

Uncertainty has much to do with the cyclical fluctuation in internal investment opportunities portrayed in Chapter IV. The notion that opportunities are much richer in prosperity is quite widespread and is understandable. The amount of added capacity needed for a current boom can be foreseen with much greater clarity than the amount needed for a dimly distant boom, and forecasts about the latter may be discounted down to nothing.

It is conceivable that when business is booming, when investment funds are plentiful, and when labor rates are rising the search for investment opportunities is more intense. As a result, more opportunities are found—but not because more are there. Cyclical changes in the optimism with which prospective profitability is viewed are probably quite pronounced and may account for much of the shift in demand schedules. This is particularly true when conjectures about the future are inadvertently or explicitly benched on an assumption that present conditions will continue indefinitely. Unless great care is taken to purge estimates of this propensity, profitability will look much better in prosperity than in depression. For example, the assumption that boom-time prices of crude petroleum and of its products would continue indefinitely was not uncommon in capital expenditure proposals in one oil company. The president had to issue a ukase that all price conjectures be based upon a ten-year historical average, rather than on the current levels in 1948, to bring about the needed deflation of profitability estimates.

SUMMARY

The desirability of stabilizing capital expenditures cyclically depends upon a balance of the gains (largely potential savings in acquisition costs) against the losses, costs, and uncertainties of long-range anticipations.

Whether it is wise to put off a capital expenditure because costs of construction or purchase are currently high depends on guesses as to how soon and how much its costs will come down in the future; estimates of how much earnings will be foregone by altering the timing disadvantageously; and estimates of the costs and losses of shifting the funds used for capital expenditures to a different point in the cycle (carrying over the retained earnings or new outside capital of a boom into the next depression or borrowing in depression in anticipation of longer-term funds from retained earnings or elsewhere).

It is impossible to avoid speculating on price level fluctuations in any effort to alter the cyclical timing of capital expenditures, and it is important to realize that whatever gains come from successful speculation are at the expense of foregone earnings and savings during the period of postponement, carrying costs during the period of anticipation, increased risks from imperfect foresight, and sometimes lost strategic opportunities.

Shrinkage of the present value of a cyclically fluctuating stream of earnings is an underlying deterrent. The difference in the present value of investment that is made in prosperity as opposed to depression is striking when discount rates are high and earnings are volatile. This deterrent is accentuated by heightened risks of obsolescence of processes and products, by imperfect foresight concerning the amount and precise embodiment of demand, and by the perishability of certain kinds of strategic opportunities.

The costs of carrying plant until needed and the higher supply price of funds in depression than in prosperity, coupled with intensified passion for cash, supplement the other deterrents and tend to dwarf the savings in acquisition costs as an inducement for stable capital formation.

Cyclical changes in uncertainties and in management's appraisal and treatment of them are to a degree an autonomous cause of cyclical fluctuations, but it is impossible to separate real uncertainties from illusions born of the disasters of the great depression. Hence, visibility of future demand and technological shifts make management's propensity to capital expenditures highly volatile. This accentuates the fluctuations inherently caused by shifts in the firm's demand and supply schedules.

The foregoing analysis has indicated that from the standpoint of the individual firm the causes of cyclical fluctuations in investment are deep-rooted and that the gains from stability are relatively small and dubious as compared with the large and certain costs and risks from departure from the pattern dictated by the shifts in the firm's scheduled demand and supply of funds. Hence, if government is to induce stable or contra-cyclical private capital formation, the incentives and compulsions must be great indeed, and if an individual firm is to do much without such changes in the rules of the game, sacrifices in earnings and loss of security will probably result.

Appendix

DISPOSAL OF ASSETS

Nature of Problem

Disposal of assets is a problem that involves the same analytical concepts employed in rationing of new capital (described in Chapter IV). In principle, it is part of the same problem, since management's basic function is to maintain a continuous surveillance of the asset package that represents the stockholders' invested capital, buying and selling properties so as to maximize the value of the firm. In practice, however, the volume of disposals is likely to be much smaller than new capital outlays, since property already owned is generally more valuable in terms of earning power than in market value. For this there are several reasons. First, some assets are specially designed for the company's purposes; second, the company knows more about the mechanical condition and performance of its equipment than others know; and, third, there are substantial transfer costs of selling in imperfect markets. As a result, assets are usually kept in the business until technical advances or changes in demand destroy their economic value for anything but scrap.

A distinction should be drawn between the problem of disposing of assets and the problem of replacing them. In a replacement investment the old equipment is not necessarily sold. It may be retained in progressively degraded service, so that the decision to replace does not stipulate disposal of the displaced asset. Moreover, replacement implies a decision to continue the activity, whereas disposal of an asset normally means discontinuance of the activity as well. Both replacements and disposals involve transfer among assets of stockholders' funds, but asset disposal is a conversion of a specialized asset into general purchasing power, while replacement involves a direct and narrow choice in transfer.

A plan for disposing of past investments is an essential part of a complete capital budgeting program. There are two ways of increasing the yield on assets by capital budgeting techniques: first, by directing the flow of new funds to projects which promise highest yield and, second, by systematic disposal of those past investments that promise lowest yield. There is danger that the disposal part of capital budgeting will be neglected. Management becomes absorbed in operating existing capital assets and develops inertia in disposing of them; moreover, there is a strong reluctance to recognize and realize capital losses through their liquidation.

But a bad investment is a source of loss; the only choice lies between immediate disposal as soon as the asset can be recognized as a "bad" investment and holding on to the asset even though it is known to be "bad." The former course of action is the more honest since the total loss is recorded upon the company's books as soon as the information is available. The latter course—holding the asset after its inferiority has been recognized—disguises the true picture by spreading the loss which has already occurred over future accounting periods and mis-labeling it as operating expense through future depreciation charges.

To be sure, the loss on a bad asset has not been "realized" in the accounting sense until the asset is sold. The loss, however, is nonetheless real in economic terms and in terms of money in the stockholder's pocket. The *book-effect* of distortion of accounting reports which will result from clinging to a bad investment is less important and less harmful than the *money-effect* which it will have upon company earnings. Failure to dispose promptly of an asset whose true economic earnings are substandard condones and preserves a mis-allocation of the stockholders' investment fund. It keeps the money tied up in unprofitable assets and prevents its reinvestment elsewhere in projects which can provide superior profit return.

The Rule

The basic principle in disposal of capital assets is that no asset should be retained if its yield is lower than the current cut-off rate required of new investments. An asset should be kept only if its yield on its current market value (i.e., disposal sale value) is high enough so that the company would want to acquire it if it did not already own it. Thus, to be complete the demand curve for capital should include the entire bundle of owned assets as well as proposed new investments, since insofar as they are marketable, existing assets compete with all new uses of the company's capital. Existing assets would be put into the demand curve at sale value with their returns computed as the ratio of expected earnings to these disposal values. Similarly, the supply curve should in theory include not only new capital—from retained earnings and the capital markets—but also already-invested capital, as measured by the sale value of owned assets as well. If new opportunities are rich, more capital funds can generally be obtained by disposing of assets of lower prospective yield.

Cost of capital provides an objective cut-off rate for disposal questions as well as for acquisition. An asset should be sold when its liquidation value is greater than its earning power capitalized at the company's cost of capital, that is, when return on liquidation value is less than cost of capital.

In practice, it is not necessary to know the complete shape of such generalized demand and supply curves, but only those segments that are close to or below the intersection point. That is, rate-of-return estimates are needed only for those assets whose profitability is suspected of falling below the cut-off standard and for those proposals that appear to be marginal.

In applying this principle, the actual rejection rate might be somewhat lower for disposals than for acquisitions because there are transfer costs of liquidation and because the profitability of existing assets can be estimated with more certainty.

The principles of estimating future annual earnings on a differential basis that were discussed in Chapter II are equally applicable in estimating the productivity of an investment that is a candidate for disposal. The decrement in total earnings through selling the asset should be compared with the incremental earnings of spending the resulting cash on alternative investments.

Amount of Investment

Disposal candidates are compared with investment proposals by expressing dollar earnings as a rate of return on the amount still tied up in the asset. To compute this productivity ratio, it is necessary to determine the value of the investment. For new investments this presents no problem, for it is the full proposed outlay. But for old investments the value is not immediately apparent.

There are three possible valuation bases:
1. Original cost at which the asset was acquired.
2. Present book value (as determined by subtracting accrued depreciation from original cost).
3. Current market value of the asset.

Of these three concepts of capital value, the first two are clearly and indisputably wrong for the purpose of capital budgeting to improve the yield on investments. Both original cost and present book value are valuation concepts altogether independent of future earnings. They represent sunk costs which have become irrevocable and over which no control can now be exercised. It is only the amount that can be recovered by selling the asset now that is relevant so far as future earnings are concerned. This current market value is a controllable cost. Management has the choice between returning that amount of money to the capital fund for reinvestment elsewhere or keeping that money tied up in the present asset. Retention of the asset, therefore, is tantamount to management's decision to invest the present market value in that asset already on the books. A decision to retain is not essentially different from a decision to re-buy, provided only that the valuation concept is economically real in the sense that the market value actually represents the amount of money which management could receive from the sale of the asset.

Relation to Accounting Values

No general reappraisal of assets is necessary under this plan for disposal of investments. Accounting valuations and book values will remain unaffected. Only those individual assets whose replacement is being studied need to be considered in the light of current market value. And for those assets the market value will be used only for the purpose of developing profitability estimates. These disposal values will not give rise to any accounting entry.

Adoption of this kind of disinvestment plan will not require any separate system of accounting or any change to conventional accounting procedures. Management will still be held accountable for results as measured by the company's present accounting valuations. This plan merely calls for assembly and presentation of the valuations and costs which are relevant for the specific management decision, namely, to sell or not to sell. These estimates are to be used for that one decision only. They will bear roughly the same relationship to the accounting and statistical records as any other form of capital budget recommendation which assembles statistical data, estimates, and accounting information for the specific purpose of deciding whether or not to buy a retail service station.

The use of the economic criteria of investments suggested here will involve some additional expense in obtaining estimates that arc actually germane. But this additional expense may be small in relation to the present accounting cost and in relation to the benefits to be received.

Relation to Managerial Accountability

The use of current market value (instead of original cost or book value) for the purpose of making a specific disinvestment decision does not in any way exonerate management for past investment errors or reduce the accountability for capital losses. On the contrary, it may serve to intensify control over capital losses because it will "highlight" capital losses and force their recognition. Casualness or indifference toward the results of investments will be far less likely than under systems in which losses are frequently "buried" and disguised as periodic overstatements of expenses in future accounting periods.

Under this scheme, management should, and can, be held fully responsible for not making bad investments in the future and for making the most out of the past investments of their predecessors. A division manager should be enabled to liquidate substandard investments and to refrain from liquidating assets which yield an adequate return as measured by the yield standard for alternative reinvestments. The fact that investments made now will subsequently be looked upon as sunk investments should not soften the criteria of initial investment or deter top management from holding divisions responsible for obtaining the profit results described in the estimate supporting the investment proposal.

It is indisputable that in a broad sense a company must ultimately be judged on the basis of its net return on total investment, so that stockholders have a right to expect an adequate return on the company's aggregate investment. But nothing in this disposal plan conflicts with such a view of investment expectations and responsibility. As measured by ratio to original investment, the earnings from capital already invested in a substandard asset will not be altered one whit by the way in which management uses the present market value of that asset as a tool to formulate an investment disposal policy which will produce the optimum decisions profits-wise. But real earnings will, in fact, be altered if management uses the wrong valuation concept and sells assets to competitors at distress prices which indicate generous earnings on current market value. The result of such action is the unnecessary loss of earnings.

The stockholders' return will likewise be unfavorably affected if the division manager is unwilling to take the disposal licking on his profit statement and holds on like grim death to assets which are not even earning a return on present market value.

Thus, this proposed disinvestment policy does not show any disregard for the orthodox methods of holding management accountable for an adequate return on total investment. Instead, it seeks to maximize that return by providing discriminatory criteria for different kinds of investment decisions.

INDEX

Accounting values, role in investment decisions, 100, 110-11, 166

Administration, *see* Management

Advertising, as capital expenditure, 4, 144

Aggressive investments, 83, 130, 141, 143-44

Assets, current, 4, 37n; amount of investment, 22, 108, 165; disposal of, 163-68

AT&T, dividend stability, 42n; control problem in financing, 57

Autonomous financing, 66-69, *chart*, 67, 159; social view, 57-59, 60

Average-minimum-cost rule, 112; Terborgh's modification, 99

"Balance," as a rationing criterion, 79

Bank loans, restrictive source of capital, 54

Bonds, factors controlling prices, 46; restrictive source of capital, 54

Bonuses, executive, as incentive to take risks, 55

Book values, *see* Accounting values

Borrowing, aversion for, 53 ff.; short-term, for contra-cyclical investments, 159

Budgeting, 2; procedure, 5; problems, 6-8; demand, 6; supply, 7; rationing: timing, 8; on annual or two-year basis, 10, 34; five-year budget, 10; excess of budget requests over available funds, 27; most important part, 38; role of cost of capital in, 43-44; capital rationing principle, 62; uses of rejection rate in admin- istrative control of, 63; long-run cut- off rate (*q.v.*), 64, 72-74; short- term, 64; ways of increasing yield on assets by, 164

Business cycles, *see* Depression; Pros- perity *and entries under* Cyclical

Capital, *see* Cost of capital; Supply of capital

Capital losses, need to recognize in disposal problems, 164

Capital market, *see* Securities market

Capital structure, relation to cost of capital, 50

Capital value, three concepts of, 166

Cash, reason for fast payback stand- ards, 27; earnings pooled, 37; fore- cast of production and disposition, 37, 38

Chrysler Corporation, growth by plow- backs, 39

Classification of expenditures, 82-88

Common stock, cost of capital in, 43, 47-48; aversion for equity financing, 56; violent changes in price-earnings ratios and dividend yields, 158

Community welfare investments, 145

Competitive entry, threat of, for new product, 136

Consumer education, a new-product investment, 136

Cost of capital, interaction of dividend policy and, 39, 41; plow-back and, 41; role in investment, 43 ff.; de- termination of company's, 44; op- portunity-cost principle, 44; market values, 45 ff.; three elements, 45;